RETIREMENT ISSUES, PLANS AND LIFESTYLES

IMPACT OF FINANCIAL CRISIS ON RETIREMENT SECURITY

RETIREMENT ISSUES, PLANS AND LIFESTYLES

Challenges Women Face In Retirement Security
Jean B. Larou
(Editor)
2009. ISBN: 978-1-60741-747-7

Social Security Reform
Aaron P. Nazario
(Editor)
2009. ISBN: 978-1-60692-275-0

Social Security Solvency
Jeffrey K. Bain
(Editor)
2009. ISBN: 978-1-60692-833-2

Financial Asset Management and Wealth in Retirement
Terrance G. Waverly
(Editor)
2010. ISBN: 978-1-60741-696-8

Impact of Financial Crisis on Retirement Security
John J. Turner
(Editor)
2010: ISBN: 978-1-60692-960-5

Impact of Financial Crisis on Retirement Security
John J. Turner
(Editor)
2010. ISBN: 978-1-61668-777-9
(E-book)

Pensions: Backgrounds, Trends and Issues
Henry J. Mullen
(Editor)
2010. ISBN: 978-1-60876-840-0

Social Security Solvency:Issues and Projections
Martin G. Roth
(Editor)
2010. ISBN: 978-1-60876-877-6

Social Security Reform: Disability, Indexing and Financing
Janet U. Burlington
(Editor)
2010. ISBN: 978-1-61668-354-2

Social Security Reform: Disability, Indexing and Financing
Janet U. Burlington
(Editor)
2010. ISBN: 978-1-61668-523-2
(E-book)

When to Retire: Issues in Working and Saving for a Secure Retirement
Maurice R. Davenworth
(Editors)
2010. ISBN: 978-1-60876-982-7

Strengthening the Retirement System Beyond Social Security
Kala E. Upshaw
(Editor)
2010. ISBN: 978-1-60741-752-1

The Role of Savings and Other Issues in Retirement Readiness
Joel K. Harris
(Editor)
2010. ISBN: 978-1-60741-446-9

Overview of the Employee Retirement Income Security Act (ERISA) - Protecting Employee Benefit Plan
Terrence D. Anderson
(Editor)
2010. ISBN: 978-1-60741-757-6

RETIREMENT ISSUES, PLANS AND LIFESTYLES

IMPACT OF FINANCIAL CRISIS ON RETIREMENT SECURITY

JOHN J. TURNER
EDITOR

Nova Science Publishers, Inc.
New York

For permission to use material from this book please contact us:
Telephone 631-231-7269; Fax 631-231-8175
Web Site: http://www.novapublishers.com

LIBRARY OF CONGRESS CATALOGING-IN-PUBLICATION DATA

Impact of financial crisis on retirement security /Editor, John J. Turner.
x, 145 p. : ill. ; 26 cm.
ISBN 978-1-60692-960-5(hardcover)
Includes bibliographical references and index.
1. Pensions --United States.2. Global Financial Crisis, 2008-2009. 3.Retirement income --United States. 4.Old age pensions --United States. I. Turner, John J.
HD7125 .I43 2010
331.2520973

2010484309

Published by Nova Science Publishers, Inc. † New York

CONTENTS

Preface		**ix**
Chapter 1	Private Pensions: Increased Reliance on 401(k) Plans Calls for Better Information on Fees *Barbara D. Bovbjerg*	**1**
Chapter 2	H.R. 3185: The 401(k) Fair Disclosure for Retirement Security Act of 2007 *John J. Topoleski*	**17**
Chapter 3	Behavioral Finance, the Market Crisis and Retirement Savings *Shlomo Benartzi*	**25**
Chapter 4	Restoring Retirement Security: The Market Crisis, the "Great Risk Shift," and the Challenge for Our Nation *Jacob S. Hacker*	**31**
Chapter 5	"The Impact of the Financial Crisis on Workers' Retirement Security" *Mark A. Davis*	**39**
Chapter 6	"The Impact of the Financial Crisis on Workers' Retirement Security" *Steve Carroll*	**45**
Chapter 7	Lessons from the Financial Crisis for Retirement Security: Building Better Retirement Plans, Testimony before the U.S. House of Representatives Committee on Education and Labor, "The Impact of the Financial Crisis on Workers' Retirement Security," October 7, 2008 *Christian E. Weller*	**47**
Chapter 8	Saving Retirement in the Face of America's Credit Crises: Short Term and Long Term Solutions, Oral Testimony, Committee on Education and Labor, "The Impact of the Financial Crisis on Workers' Retirement Security," Rayburn House Office Building, Tuesday, October 7, 2008 *Teresa Ghilarducci, Irene Schwartz and Bernard L. Schwartz*	**65**

Chapter 9 The Effects of Recent Turmoil in Financial Markets on Retirement Security before the Committee on Education and Labor, U.S. House of Representatives **73**
Peter R. Orszag

Chapter 10 Testimony for the House Education and Labor Committee, "The Impact of the Financial Crisis on Workers' Retirement Security," October 7, 2008 **81**
Jack VanDerhei

Chapter 11 Statement by Roberta Tim Quan, U.S. House Committee on Education and Labor, George Miller "The Impact of the Financial Crisis on Workers' Retirement Security," October 22, 2008 **87**
Roberta Tim Quan

Chapter 12 Statement by Jerry Bramlett, BenefitStreet, Inc., Comments Presented to the House Education and Labor Committee, U.S. House of Representatives "The Impact of the Financial Crisis on Workers' Retirement Security," October 7, 2008 **89**
Jerry Bramlett

Chapter 13 Chairman Miller Statement at Committee Hearing on "The Impact of the Financial Crisis on Workers' Retirement Security," October 22, 2008 **93**
Education and Labor Committee

Chapter 14 Chairman Miller Statement at Committee Hearing on "The Impact of the Financial Crisis on Workers' Retirement Security," October 7, 2008 **97**
Education and Labor Committee

Chapter 15 Written Testimony of Matthew D. Hutcheson, Independent Pension Fiduciary on "Are Hidden Fees Undermining Employee Retirement Income Security?" Presented to the Committee on Education and Labor, U.S. House of Representatives, March 6, 2007 **101**
Matthew D. Hutcheson

Chapter 16 Written Testimony of Stephen J. Butler, President of Pension Dynamics Corporations, Author and Weekly Financial Columnist on "Undermining Workers' Retirement Security," presented to the Committee on Education and Labor, U.S. House of Representatives **123**
Stephen J. Butler

Chapter 17 The 401(k) Fair Disclosure for Retirement Security Act - Myths v. Facts **135**
John J. Turner

Index **137**

PREFACE

The long-term trend in declining retirement security has been exacerbated by the recent turmoil in the financial markets, and underscores the need for swift and broad action to vastly improve the retirement income security for the majority of American families. Americans need to be reassured that the money that they will save for retirement will actually be there when they need it. The exposure to large market swings, as people have experienced twice in the past decade, can send individual investors scrambling for an exit at the most inopportune time. This prevents them from saving enough, and actually increases their exposure to financial market risks. This book examines the impact and issues of the financial crisis on retirement security in the United States. This book consists of public documents which have been located, gathered, combined, reformatted, and enhanced with a subject index, selectively edited and bound to provide easy access.

Chapter 1 - Over the past two decades there has been a noticeable shift in the types of plans employers are offering employees. Employers are increasingly moving away from traditional defined benefit plans to what has become the most dominant and fastest growing type of defined contribution plan, the 401(k).

As more workers participate in 401(k) plans, they bear more of the responsibility for funding their retirement. Given the choices facing participants, specific information about the plan and plan options becomes more relevant than under defined benefit plans because participants are responsible for ensuring that they have adequate income at retirement. While information on historical performance and investment risk for each plan option are important for participants to understand, so too is information on fees because fees can significantly decrease participants' retirement savings over the course of a career. As a result of employees bearing more responsibility for funding their retirement under 401(k) plans, you asked us to talk about the prevalence of 401(k) plans today and to summarize the authors' recent work on providing better information to 401(k) participants and the Department of Labor (Labor) on fees. My remarks today will focus on (1) trends in the use of 401(k) plans, and (2) the types of fees associated with these plans.

Chapter 2 - As households become more reliant on 401(k) plans for retirement income, policymakers have become more concerned that participants are unaware of the fees charged in their 401(k) plans. Small differences in fees charged can have large impacts on 401(k) account balances upon retirement. This report provides information on the kinds of fees that are charged in 401(k) plans and details the provisions of H.R. 3185, the 401(k) Fair Disclosure for Retirement Security Act as introduced on July 14, 2007. was passed by the Committee on Education and Labor by a vote of 25-19 on April 16, 2008. It will updated to reflect other 401(k) fee disclosure legislation.

Chapters 3, 4, 5, 6, 7, 8, 9, 10, 11, 12, 13, 14, 15 and 16 feature testimony before the U. S. House of Representatives.

Chapter 17 features myths and facts about 401(k) plans.

In: Impact of Financial Crisis on Retirement Security
Editor: John J. Turner

ISBN: 978-1-60692-960-5

Chapter 1

PRIVATE PENSIONS: INCREASED RELIANCE ON 401(K) PLANS CALLS FOR BETTER INFORMATION ON FEES*

Barbara D. Bovbjerg

WHY GAO DID THIS STUDY

Over the past two decades there has been a noticeable shift in the types of plans employers are offering employees. Employers are increasingly moving away from traditional defined benefit plans to what has become the most dominant and fastest growing type of defined contribution plan, the 401(k).

As more workers participate in 401(k) plans, they bear more of the responsibility for funding their retirement. Given the choices facing participants, specific information about the plan and plan options becomes more relevant than under defined benefit plans because participants are responsible for ensuring that they have adequate income at retirement. While information on historical performance and investment risk for each plan option are important for participants to understand, so too is information on fees because fees can significantly decrease participants' retirement savings over the course of a career. As a result of employees bearing more responsibility for funding their retirement under 401(k) plans, you asked us to talk about the prevalence of 401(k) plans today and to summarize our recent work on providing better information to 401(k) participants and the Department of Labor (Labor) on fees. My remarks today will focus on (1) trends in the use of 401(k) plans, and (2) the types of fees associated with these plans.

* This is an edited, reformatted and augmented version of a U. S. Government Accountability Office publication dated March 2007.

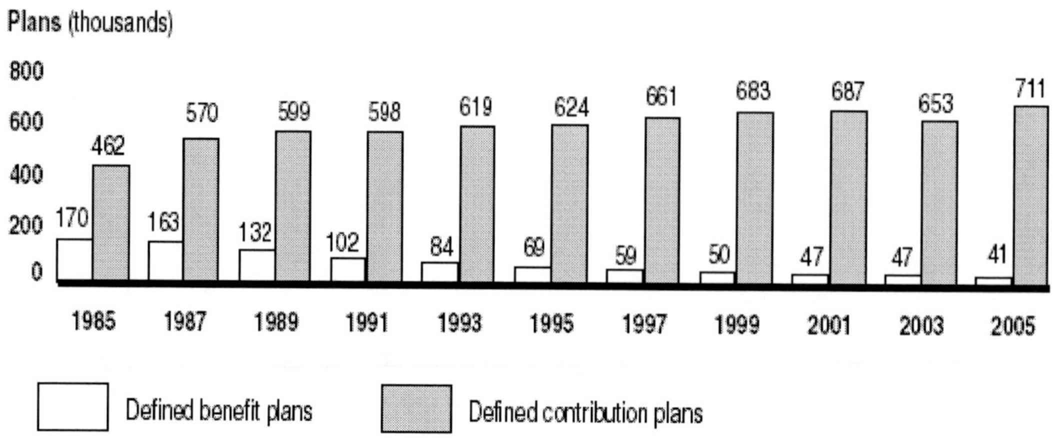

Source: U.S. Department of Labor (1985 - 2003 data); Investment Company Institute (2005 estimates).

Comparison of Defined Benefit Plans with Defined Contribution Plans, 1985 and 2005

WHAT GAO FOUND

There are an increasing number of active participants in 401(k) plans than in other types of employer-sponsored pension plans, a trend that has accelerated since the 1980s. Now, 401(k) plans represent the majority of all private pension plans; they also service the most participants and hold the most assets. These plans offer a range of investment options, but equity funds—those that invest primarily in stocks—accounted for nearly half of 401(k) assets at the close of 2005. Most 401(k) plans are participant-directed, meaning that a participant is responsible for making the investment decisions about his or her own retirement plan contributions.

Inadequate disclosure and reporting requirements may leave participants without a simple way to compare fees among plan investment options, and Labor without the information it needs to oversee fees and identify questionable 401(k) business practices. The Employee Retirement Income Security Act (ERISA) of 1974 requires 401(k) plan sponsors to disclose only limited information on fees. Participants must collect various documents over time and may be required to seek out some documents in order to get a clear picture of the total fees that they pay. Furthermore, the documents that participants receive do not provide a simple way to compare fees—along with risk and historical performance—among the investment options in their 401(k) plan. The information reported to Labor does not identify all fees charged to 401(k) plans and therefore has limited use for effectively overseeing fees and identifying undisclosed business arrangements among consultants or service providers. As a result, participants may have more limited investment options and pay higher fees for these options than they otherwise would.

Mr. Chairman and Members of the Committee:

I am pleased to be here to discuss American workers' increased participation in 401(k) plans and the potential effects of the fees associated with these plans on their retirement income. Over the past two decades there has been a noticeable shift in the types of plans employers are offering employees. Employers are increasingly moving away from traditional defined benefit plans to what has become the most dominant and fastest growing type of defined contribution plan, the 401(k).[1]

As more workers participate in 401(k) plans, they bear more of the responsibility for funding their retirement than they do when covered by traditional defined benefit plans. Under 401(k) plans, participants are responsible for choosing how much of their pretax income to contribute, how to invest their contributions in the choices offered by the plan sponsor, and how to manage their 401(k) investments upon retirement. Given the choices facing participants, specific information about the plan and plan options becomes more relevant than under defined benefit plans because participants are responsible for ensuring that they have adequate income at retirement. Although information on historical performance and investment risk for each plan option are important for participants to understand, so too is information on fees because fees can significantly decrease participants' retirement savings over the course of a career. As a result of employees bearing more responsibility for funding their retirement under 401(k) plans, you asked us to talk about the prevalence of 401(k) plans in the private pension system today and to summarize our recent work on providing better information to 401(k) participants and the Department of Labor (Labor) on fees. My remarks today will focus on (1) trends in the use of 401(k) plans, and (2) the types of fees associated with these plans and the information available to participants and Labor.

To describe the current trend toward the increased use of 401(k) plans, we relied on our previous work on the nature of the private pension system and information from Labor and industry research. Regarding plan fees, we also relied on our previous work that looked at the types of fees associated with 401(k) plans, who pays these fees, how information is disclosed to participants, and Labor's oversight of fees and certain related business arrangements.[2] We conducted our review from February 2007 through March 2007 in accordance with generally accepted government auditing standards.

In summary, there are more active participants now in 401(k) plans than other types of employer-sponsored pension plans, a trend that has accelerated since the 1980s.[3] Now, 401(k) plans represent the majority of all private pension plans; they also service the most participants and hold the most assets. These plans offer a range of investment options, but equity funds—those that invest primarily in stocks—accounted for nearly half of 401(k) assets at the close of 2005. Most 401(k) plans are participant-directed, meaning that a participant is responsible for making the investment decisions about his or her own retirement plan contributions.

Inadequate disclosure and reporting requirements may leave participants without a simple way to compare fees among plan investment options, and Labor without the information it needs to oversee fees and identify questionable 401(k) business practices. The Employee Retirement Income Security Act of 1974 (ERISA)[4] requires 401(k) plan sponsors to disclose only limited information on fees. Participants must collect various documents over time and may be required to seek out some documents in order to get a clear picture of the total fees that they pay. Furthermore, the documents that participants receive do not provide a simple way to compare fees—along with risk and historical performance—among the investment options in their 401(k) plan. The information reported to Labor does not identify all fees charged to 401(k) plans and therefore has limited use for effectively overseeing fees and identifying undisclosed business arrangements among consultants or service providers. As a result, participants may have more limited investment options and pay higher fees for these options than they otherwise would.

BACKGROUND

Roughly half of all workers participate in an employer-sponsored retirement, or pension plan. Private sector pension plans are classified as either defined benefit or defined contribution plans. Defined benefit plans promise to provide, generally, a fixed level of monthly retirement income that is based on salary, years of service, and age at retirement regardless of how the plan's investments perform. In contrast, benefits from defined contribution plans are based on the contributions to and the performance of the investments in individual accounts, which may fluctuate in value. Examples of defined contribution plans include 401(k) profit-sharing and thrift-savings plans, stock bonus plans, and annuity plans.

Labor's Employee Benefits Security Administration (EBSA) oversees 401(k) plans— including the fees associated with running the plans— because they are considered employee benefit plans under ERISA. Enacted before 401(k) plans came into wide use, ERISA establishes the responsibilities of employee benefit plan decision makers and the requirements for disclosing and reporting plan fees. Typically, the plan sponsor is a fiduciary.[5] A plan fiduciary includes a person who has discretionary control or authority over the management or administration of the plan, including the plan's assets. ERISA requires that plan sponsors responsible for managing employee benefit plans carry out their responsibilities prudently and do so solely in the interest of the plans' participants and beneficiaries.

The law also provides Labor with oversight authority over pension plans.[6] However, the specific investment products commonly contained in pension plans—such as company stock, mutual funds, collective investment funds, and group annuity contracts—fall under the authority of the applicable securities, banking, or insurance regulators:

- The Securities and Exchange Commission (SEC), among other responsibilities, regulates registered securities including company stock and mutual funds under securities law.[7]
- The federal agencies charged with oversight of banks—primarily the Federal Reserve Board, the Treasury Department's Office of the Comptroller of the Currency, and the Federal Deposit Insurance Corporation—regulate bank investment products, such as collective investment funds.
- State agencies generally regulate insurance products, such as variable annuity contracts. Such investment products may also include one or more insurance elements, which are not present in other investment options. Generally, these elements include an annuity feature, interest and expense guarantees, and any death benefit provided during the term of the contract.[8]

AN INCREASING NUMBER OF EMPLOYEES PARTICIPATE IN DEFINED CONTRIBUTION PLANS, AND THIS TREND HAS BEEN INCREASING SINCE THE 1980S

The number of defined contribution plans has increased since 1985, while the number of defined benefit plans has declined dramatically.[9] Figure 1 shows the growth of defined contribution plans relative to that of defined benefit plans from 1985 to 2005.

In 2005, more workers were covered by defined contribution plans than by defined benefit plans. In 1985, defined benefit plans covered approximately 29 million active participants, compared to 33 million active participants in defined contribution plans. By 2005, the difference in the numbers had become more pronounced, with roughly 21 million active participants covered by defined benefit plans and approximately 55 million active participants in defined contribution plans. Figure 2 shows the shift in active participants from defined benefit to defined contribution plans since 1985.

With the growth in plans and participants, the majority of private pension plan assets are now held in defined contribution plans. As shown in figure 3, defined benefit plan assets decreased from $2.0 trillion in constant 2006 dollars, or about 66 percent of total private pension assets, in 1985 to $1.5 trillion, or just over 40 percent of the total, in 2005.[10]

Similarly, the number of 401(k) plans grew from less than 30,000 in 1985, or less than 7 percent of all defined contribution plans, to an estimated 417,000 plans, or about 95 percent of all defined contribution plans in 2005. During this same time period, the number of active participants in 40 1(k) plans increased from 10 million to 47 million, and plan assets increased from $270 billion to about $2.5 trillion in constant 2006 dollars.

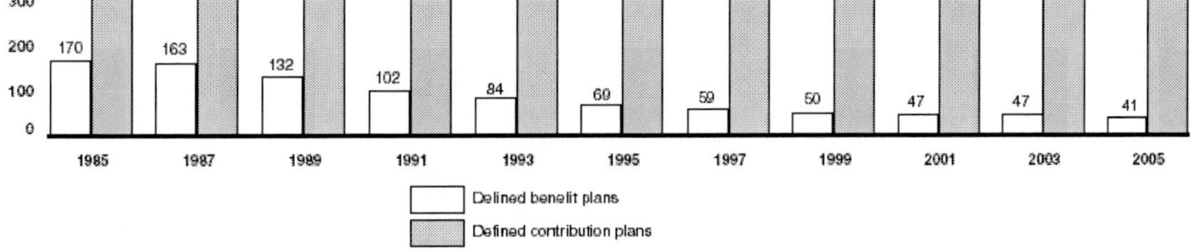

Source: U.S. Department of Labor (1985 - 2003 data); Investment Company Institute (2005 estimates).
Note: The Investment Company Institute's estimates for 2005 are based on the Department of Labor, Form 5500 Annual Reports, and other information.

Figure 1. Changes in the Number of Defined Benefit Plans and Defined Contribution Plans, 1985-2005

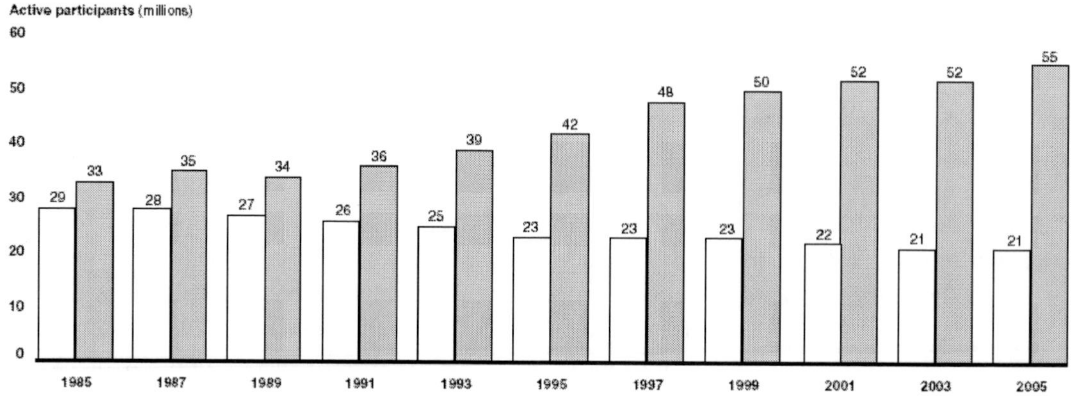

Source: U.S. Department of Labor (1985 - 2003 data); Investment Company Institute (2005 estimates).
Note: The Investment Company Institute's estimates for 2005 are based on the Department of Labor, Form 5500 Annual Reports, and other information.

Figure 2. Changes in the Number of Active Participants in Defined Benefit Plans and Defined Contribution Plans, 1985-2005

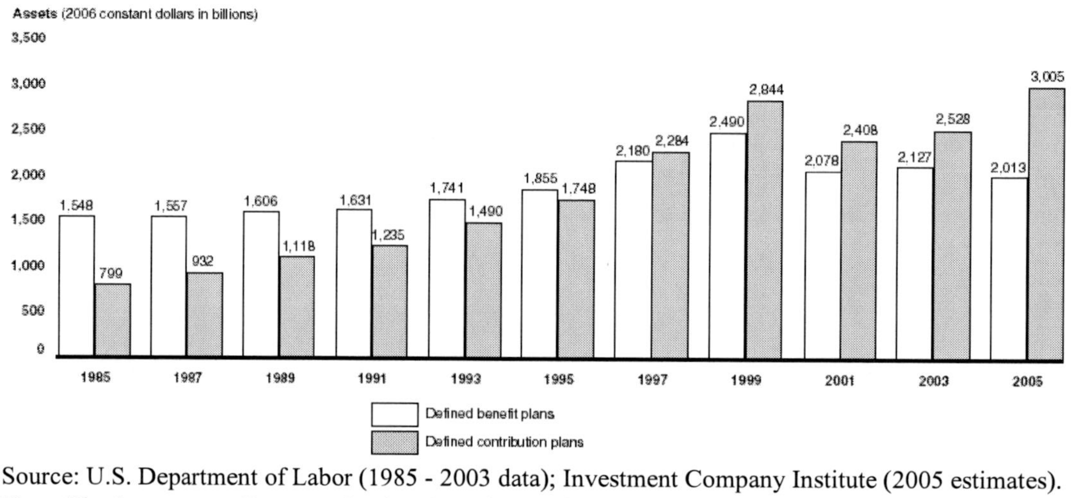

Source: U.S. Department of Labor (1985 - 2003 data); Investment Company Institute (2005 estimates).
Note: The Investment Company Institute's estimates for 2005 are based on the Department of Labor, Form 5500 Annual Reports, and other information.

Figure 3. Changes in Defined Benefit and Defined Contribution Plan Assets, 1985-2005

Based on industry estimates, equity funds accounted for nearly half of the 401(k) plan assets at the close of 2005.[11] Equity funds are investment options that invest primarily in stocks, such as mutual funds, bank collective funds,[12] life insurance separate accounts, and certain pooled investment products (see figure 4). Other plan assets were invested in company stock; stable value funds,[13] including guaranteed investment contracts; balanced funds;[14] bond funds; and money funds. Several of these options can be held in mutual funds, which in total represent about 51 percent of 401(k) plan assets. Common plan features, like the type and number of investment options provided to participants in their 401(k) plans, is a topic being studied under other GAO work on plan sponsor practices requested by this committee.

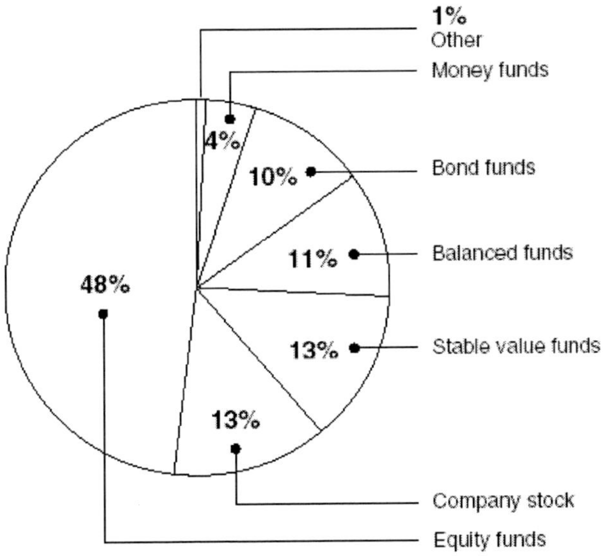

Source: Investment Company Institute.

Note: The Investment Company Institute's estimates for 2005 are based on the Department of Labor, Form 5500 Annual Reports; and other information

Figure 4. 401(k) Plan Average Asset Allocation in 2005

With the growth in 401(k) plans, more workers now bear greater responsibility for funding their retirement income. According to the most recent data from Labor, the majority of 401(k) plans are participant- directed, meaning that a participant makes investment decisions about his or her own retirement plan contributions. In 2003, about 88 percent of all 401(k) plans—covering 93 percent of all active 401(k) plan participants and 92 percent of all 401(k) plan assets—generally allowed participants to choose how much to invest, within federal limits, and to select from a menu of diversified investment options selected by the employer sponsoring the plan.[15]

While some participants have account balances of greater than $100,000, most have much smaller balances. Based on industry estimates for 2005, 37 percent of participants had balances of less than $10,000, while 16 percent had balances greater than $100,000.[16] The median account balance was $19,328, while the average account balance was $58,328. Participants' account balances also include any contributions employers make on their behalf.

Fees are charged by the various outside companies that the plan sponsor—often the employer offering the 401(k) plan—hires to provide a number of services necessary to operate the plan. Services can include investment management (i.e., selecting and managing the securities included in a mutual fund); consulting and providing financial advice (i.e., selecting vendors for investment options or other services); record keeping (i.e., tracking individual account contributions); custodial or trustee services for plan assets (i.e., holding the plan assets in a bank); and telephone or Web-based customer services for participants. Generally there are two ways to provide services: "bundled" (the sponsor hires one company that provides the full range of services directly or through subcontracts) and "unbundled" (the sponsor uses a combination of service providers).

Fees are one of many factors—such as the historical performance and investment risk for each plan option—participants should consider when investing in a 401(k) plan because fees can significantly decrease retirement savings over the course of a career. As participants accrue earnings on their investments, they pay a number of fees, including expenses, commissions, or other charges associated with operating a 401(k) plan. Over the course of the employee's career, for example, a 1 percentage point difference in fees can significantly reduce the amount of money saved for retirement. Figure 5 assumes an employee who is 45 years of age with 20 years until retirement changes employers and leaves $20,000 in a 401(k) account until retirement. If the average annual net return is 6.5 percent—a 7 percent investment return minus a 0.5 percent charge for fees—the $20,000 will grow to about $70,500 at retirement. However, if fees are instead 1.5 percent annually, the average net return is reduced to 5.5 percent, and the $20,000 will grow to only about $58,400. The additional 1 percent annual charge for fees would reduce the account balance at retirement by about 17 percent.

INVESTMENT AND RECORD-KEEPING FEES ACCOUNT FOR MOST 401(K) PLAN FEES, BUT INFORMATION ON THESE FEES MAY BE LIMITED OR UNAVAILABLE TO PARTICIPANTS AND LABOR

Various fees are associated with 401(k) plans, but investment and record-keeping fees account for most 401(k) plan fees. However, inadequate disclosure and reporting requirements may leave participants and Labor without important information on these fees. The information on fees that plan sponsors are required to disclose to participants does not allow participants to easily compare the fees for the investment options in their 401(k) plan. In addition, Labor does not have the information it needs to oversee fees and identify questionable 401(k) business practices. Labor has several initiatives under way to improve the information it has on fees and the various business arrangements among service providers.

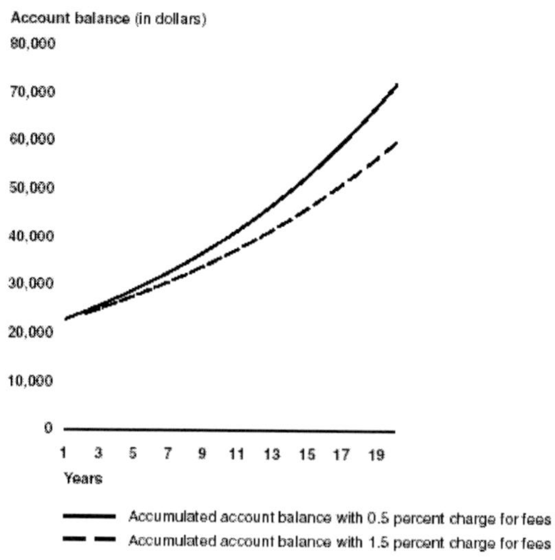

Source: GAO analysis.

Figure 5. Effect of 1 Percentage Point in Higher Annual Fees on a $20,000 401(k) Balance Invested over 20 Years

Investment Fees Account for Most 401(k) Plan Fees and Are Usually Borne by Plan Participants

Investment fees account for the largest portion of total fees regardless of plan size, as figure 6 illustrates. Investment fees are, for example, fees charged by companies that manage a mutual fund for all services related to operating the fund. These fees pay for selecting a mutual fund's portfolio of securities and managing the fund; marketing the fund and compensating brokers who sell the fund; and providing other shareholder services, such as distributing the fund prospectus.

Plan record-keeping fees generally constitute the second-largest portion of plan fees. Plan record-keeping fees are usually charged by the service provider to set up and maintain the 40 1(k) plan. These fees cover activities such as enrolling plan participants, processing participant fund selections, preparing and mailing account statements, and other related administrative activities. Unlike investment fees, plan record-keeping fees apply to the entire 401(k) plan rather than the individual investment options. As shown in figure 7, these fees make up a smaller proportion of total plan fees in larger plans, indicating economies of scale.

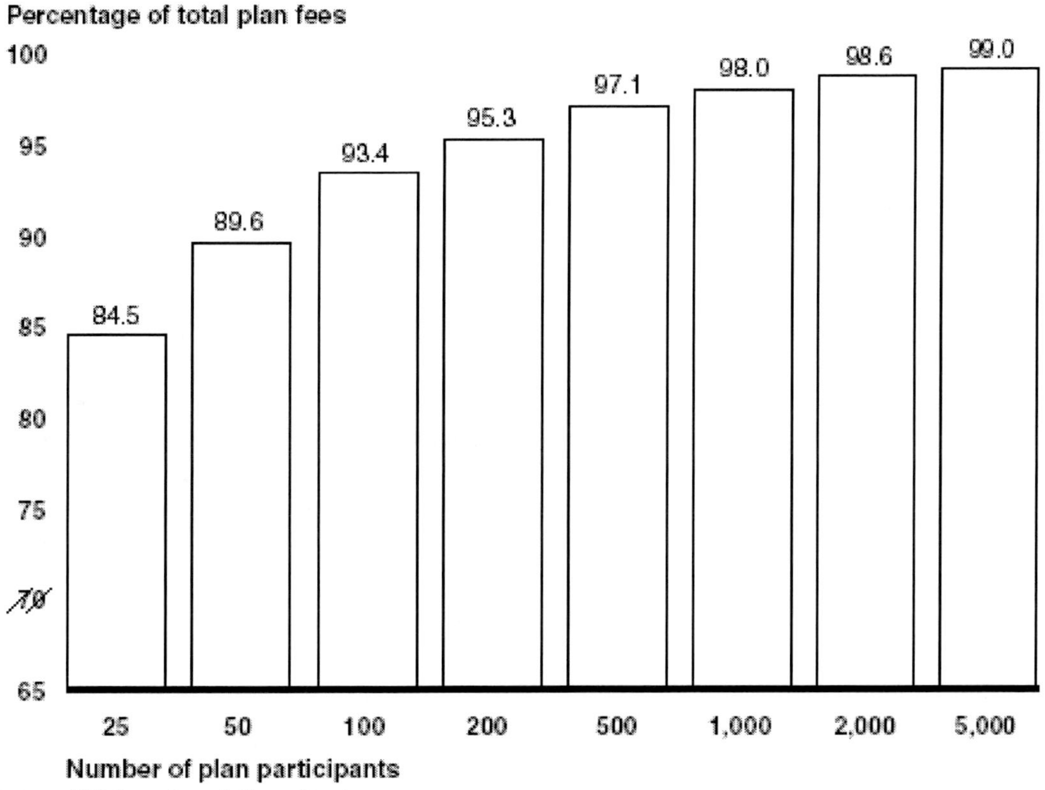

Source: HR Investment Consultants.

Note: The results of HR Investment Consultants' survey are based on responses from 125 vendors that service 401(k) plans. This response represents about 85 percent of the assets invested in 401(k) plans but may not be representative of the universe of 401(k) plans.

Figure 6. Investment Fees as a Percentage of Total Plan Fees, 2005

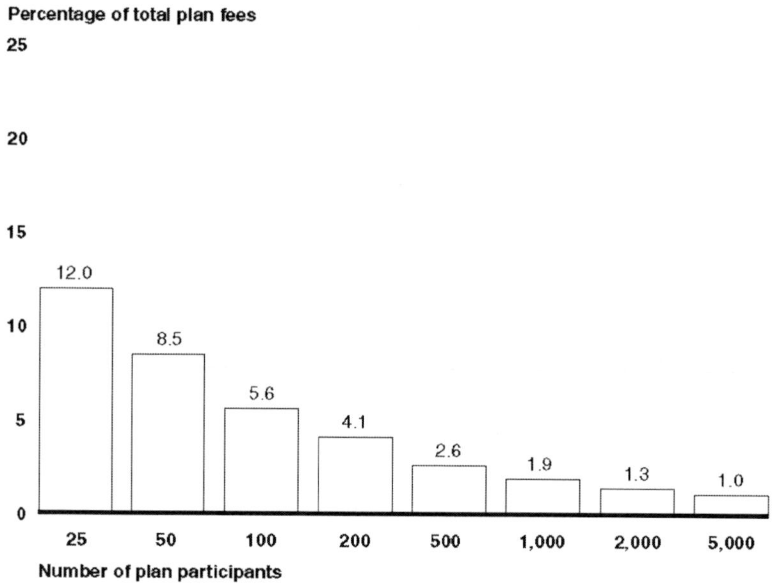

Source: HR Investment Consultants.

Note: The results of HR Investment Consultants' survey are based on responses from 125 vendors that service 401(k) plans. This response represents about 85 percent of the assets invested in 401(k) plans but may not be representative of the universe of 401(k) plans. While these data include primarily record keeping, they include a negligible amount of other administrative fees, according to the survey author.

Figure 7. Plan Record-Keeping Fees as a Percentage of Total Plan Fees, 2005

There are a number of other fees associated with establishing and maintaining a plan, such as fees to communicate basic information about the plan to participants. However, these fees generally constitute a much smaller percentage of total plan fees than investment and plan record- keeping fees.

Whether and how participants or plan sponsors pay these fees varies by the type of fee and the size of the 401(k) plan. Investment fees, which are usually charged as a fixed percentage of assets and deducted from investment returns, are typically borne by participants. Plan record- keeping fees are charged as a percentage of a participant's assets, a flat fee, or a combination of both. Although plan sponsors pay these fees in a considerable number of plans, they are increasingly being paid by participants.

Required Disclosures Provide Limited Fee Information to Assist Participants in Comparing Investment Options

ERISA requires that plan sponsors provide all participants with a summary plan description, account statements, and the summary annual report, but these documents are not required to disclose information on fees borne by individual participants. Table 1 provides an overview of each of these disclosure documents, and the type of fee information they may contain.

Table 1. Required Disclosure Documents to All Participants

Disclosure document	Document purpose	Information on fees
Summary plan description	To explain to participants how the plan operates	May contain information on how various fees such as investment, record-keeping, and loan fees are charged to participants, but not required by ERISA to do so.
Account statement	To show the account balance due to a participant	Typically identifies fees, such as for loans, which are directly attributable to an account during a specific period. Also, may show investment and record-keeping fees, but not required by ERISA to do so.
Summary annual report	To disclose the financial condition of the plan to participants	Contains total plan costs incurred by plan participants during the year.

Source: GAO analysis.

ERISA also requires 401(k) plan sponsors that have elected liability protection from participants' investment decisions to provide additional fee information.[17] Most 401(k) plan sponsors elect this protection and therefore must provide, among other information, a description of the investment risk and historical performance of each investment option available in the plan and any associated transaction fees for buying or selling shares in these options. Upon request, these plans must also provide participants with the expense ratio—a fund's operating fees as a percentage of its assets—for each investment option.

Plan sponsors may voluntarily provide participants with more information on fees than ERISA requires. For example, plans may distribute prospectuses or fund profiles for individual investment options in the plan. Although not required, plan sponsors may provide record-keeping or other information on fees in participants' account statements.

Although participants are responsible for directing their investments in the plan, they may not be aware of the different fees that they pay. In a nationwide survey, more than 80 percent of 401(k) participants report not knowing how much they pay in fees.[18] Some industry professionals said that making participants who direct their investments more aware of fees would help them make more informed investment decisions.

Participants may not have a clear picture of the total fees they pay because plan sponsors provide this information in a piecemeal fashion. Some documents that contain fee information are provided to participants automatically, such as annually or within 90 days of joining the plan, while others, such as prospectuses, may require that participants seek them out.

Furthermore, the documents that participants receive do not provide a simple way for participants to compare fees among the investment options in their 401(k) plan. Industry professionals suggested that comparing the expense ratio across investment options is the most effective way to compare fees within a 401(k) plan.[19] The expense ratio is useful because it includes investment fees, which account for most of the fees participants pay, and is generally the only fee measure that varies by option. However, as noted above, not all plan sponsors are required to provide expense ratios to participants.

Labor Has Authority over 401(k) Plan Fees and Certain Types of Business Arrangements, but Lacks Information for Effective Oversight

Labor has authority under ERISA to oversee 401(k) plan fees and certain types of business arrangements involving service providers, but lacks the information it needs to provide effective oversight. Under ERISA, Labor is responsible for enforcing the requirements that plan sponsors (1) ensure that fees paid with plan assets are reasonable and for necessary services; (2) be prudent and diversify the plan's investments or, if plan sponsors elect liability protection, provide a broad range of investment choices for participants; and (3) report information known on certain business arrangements involving service providers. Labor does this in a number of ways, including collecting some information on fees from plan sponsors, investigating participants' complaints or referrals from other agencies on questionable 401(k) plan practices, and conducting outreach to educate plan sponsors about their responsibilities.

However, the information plan sponsors are required to report to Labor is limited, and the lack of information hinders the agency's ability to effectively oversee fees. Many of the fees are associated with the individual investment options in the 401(k) plan, such as a mutual fund; they are deducted from investment returns and not included on the annual reporting form plan sponsors submit to Labor, Form 5500. As a result, the Form 5500 does not include the largest type of fee, even though plan sponsors receive this information from the mutual fund companies in the form of a prospectus. In 2004, the ERISA Advisory Council concluded that Form 5500s are of little use to policy makers, government enforcement personnel, and participants in terms of understanding the cost of a plan and recommended that Labor modify the form and its accompanying schedules so that all fees incurred directly or indirectly can be reported or estimated. Without information on all fees, Labor's oversight is limited because it is unable to identify fees that may be questionable.

Labor and plan sponsors also may not have information on arrangements among service providers that could steer plan sponsors toward offering investment options that benefit service providers but may not be in the best interest of participants. For example, the SEC released a report in May 2005 that raised questions about whether some pension consultants are fully disclosing potential conflicts of interest that may affect the objectivity of the advice.[20] Plan sponsors pay pension consultants to give them advice on matters such as selecting investment options for the plan and monitoring their performance and selecting other service providers, such as custodians, administrators, and broker-dealers. The report highlighted concerns that these arrangements may provide incentives for pension consultants to recommend certain mutual funds to a 401(k) plan sponsor and create conflicts of interest that are not adequately disclosed to plan sponsors. Plan sponsors may not be aware of these arrangements and thus could select mutual funds recommended by the pension consultant over lower-cost alternatives. As a result, participants may have more limited investment options and may pay higher fees for these options than they otherwise would.

In addition, specific fees that are considered to be "hidden" may mask the existence of a conflict of interest. Hidden fees are usually related to business arrangements where one service provider to a 401(k) plan pays a third-party provider for services, such as record keeping, but does not disclose this compensation to the plan sponsor. For example, a mutual fund normally provides record-keeping services for its retail investors, i.e., those who invest outside of a 401(k) plan. The same mutual fund, when associated with a plan, might compensate the plan's record keeper for performing the services that it would otherwise perform, such as maintaining individual participants' account records and consolidating their requests to buy or sell shares.[21]

The problem with hidden fees is not how much is being paid to the service provider, but with knowing what entity is receiving the compensation and whether or not the compensation fairly represents the value of the service being rendered. Labor's position is that plan sponsors must know about these fees in order to fulfill their fiduciary responsibilities. However, if the plan sponsors do not know that a third party is receiving these fees, they cannot monitor them, evaluate the worthiness of the compensation in view of services rendered, and take action as needed.

Labor Has Several Initiatives under Way to Improve Information It Has on Fees and the Various Business Arrangements among Service Providers

Labor officials told us about three initiatives currently under way to improve the disclosure of fee information by plan sponsors to participants and to avoid conflicts of interest:

- Labor is considering promulgating a rule regarding the fee information required to be furnished to participants in plans where sponsors have elected liability protection. According to Labor officials, they are attempting to define the critical information on fees that plan sponsors should provide to participants and what format would enable participants to easily compare the fees across the plan's various investment options.
- Labor has proposed changes to the Form 5500 Schedule A and Schedule C to improve reporting of fees.[22]
    - Labor proposed to add a check box on Schedule A to improve the disclosure of insurance fees and commissions and identify insurers who fail to supply information to plan sponsors. According to a 2004 ERISA Advisory Council report,[23] many employers have difficulty obtaining timely Schedule A information from insurers.
    - Consistent with recommendations made by the ERISA Advisory Council Working Groups and GAO, Labor proposed changes to the Schedule C to clarify that the plan sponsor must report any direct and indirect compensation (i.e., money or anything else of value) it pays to a service provider during the plan year. Plan sponsors also would be required to disclose the source and nature of compensation in excess of $1,000 that certain key service providers, including, among others, investment managers, consultants, brokers, and trustees as well as all other fiduciaries, receive from parties other than the plan or the plan sponsor, such as record keepers. Labor officials told us that the revision aims to improve the information plan sponsors receive from service providers. The officials acknowledge, however, that this requirement may be difficult for plan sponsors to fulfill without an explicit requirement in ERISA for service providers to give plan sponsors information on the fees they pay to other providers.

- The third initiative involves amending Labor's regulations under section 408(b)(2) of ERISA to define the information plan sponsors need in deciding whether to select or retain a service provider. According to Labor, plan sponsors need information to assess the reasonableness of the fees being paid by the plan for services rendered and to assess potential conflicts of interest that might affect the objectivity with which the service provider provides its services to the plan. This change to the regulation would be intended to make clear what plan sponsors need to know and, accordingly, what service providers need to provide to plan sponsors.

To ensure that participants have a tool to make informed comparisons and decisions among plan investment options, we recommended in our previous report that Congress consider amending ERISA to require all sponsors of participant-directed plans to disclose fee information of 401(k) investment options to participants in a way that facilitates comparison among the options. To better enable the agency to effectively oversee 401(k) plan fees, we recommended that the Secretary of Labor should require plan sponsors to report a summary of all fees that are paid out of plan assets or by participants. To allow plan sponsors, and ultimately Labor, to provide better oversight of fees and certain business arrangements among service providers, we also recommended that Congress should consider amending ERISA to explicitly require that 401(k) service providers disclose to plan sponsors the compensation that providers receive from other service providers. In response to our draft report, Labor generally agreed with our findings and conclusions. Specifically, Labor stated that it will give careful consideration to GAO's recommendation that plans be required to provide a summary of all fees that are paid out of plan assets or by participants. Labor and SEC also provided technical comments on the draft, which we incorporated as appropriate.

Conclusion

The pension plan universe has changed: 401(k) plans have emerged to cover most plan participants and the majority of plan assets. With this shift, participants now bear more responsibility for ensuring they have adequate income in retirement, emphasizing the importance of having sufficient information to make informed 401(k) investment decisions. Information about investment options' historical performance is useful, but alone is not enough. Thus, giving participants key information on fees for each of the plan's investment options in a simple format—including fees, historical performance, and risk—will help participants make informed investment decisions within their 401(k) plan. In choosing between investment options with similar performance and risk profiles but different fee structures, the additional provision of expense ratio data may help participants build their retirement savings over time by avoiding investments with relatively high fees.

Regulators, too, will need to have better information to provide more effective oversight, especially of the fees associated with 401(k) plans. Amending ERISA and updating regulations to better reflect the impact of fees and undisclosed business arrangements among service providers will help put Labor in a better position to oversee 401(k) plan fees. Furthermore, requiring plan sponsors to report more complete information to Labor on fees—

those paid out of plan assets or by participants—would put the agency in a better position to effectively oversee 401(k) plans.

End Notes

[1] Traditional defined benefit plans generally provide a fixed level of monthly retirement income that is based on salary, years of service, and age at retirement regardless of how the plan's investments perform. In contrast, benefits from defined contribution plans are based on the contributions to and the performance of the investments in individual accounts, which may fluctuate in value.

[2] GAO, *PRIVATE PENSIONS: Changes Needed To Provide 401(k) Plan Participants and the Department of Labor Better Information on Fees*, GAO-07-21 (Washington, D.C.: Nov. 2006).

[3] Active participants include any worker currently in employment covered by a plan and workers who are earning or retaining credited service under a plan. It does not include retired participants and vested participants not yet in pay status.

[4] 29 U.S.C. §§ 100 1-1461.

[5] A plan fiduciary is anyone who exercises discretionary authority or control over plan management (or any authority or control over the management or distribution of plan assets), renders or is responsible for rendering investment advice for a fee, or has discretionary authority or responsibility in plan administration. 29 U.S.C. § 1002(21)(A).

[6] The Internal Revenue Service also oversees various aspects of 401(k) contributions under the authority of the Internal Revenue Code. Roth contributions to 401(k) plans were created under the Economic Growth and Tax Relief Reconciliation Act of 2001 effective for plan years beginning on or after January 1, 2006. This new account type was subsequently made permanent under the Pension Protection Act of 2006. Designated Roth contributions are a new type of contribution that can be accepted by new or existing 401(k) plans. If a plan adopts this feature, employees can designate some or all of their elective contributions as Roth contributions (which are included in gross income) rather than pretax elective contributions.

[7] 15 U.S.C. § 78a. Generally, public offerings and the sale of securities must be registered with the SEC.

[8] The variable annuity contract "wraps" around investment options, often a number of mutual funds. Participants select from among the investment options offered, and the return to their individual accounts varies with their choice of investments. If registered securities make up the underlying investments, they are regulated by the SEC.

[9] For 1985 data, see "Private Pension Plan Bulletin Abstract of 1999 Form 5500 Annual Reports," U.S. Department of Labor (1985 data); for 2005 estimates, see Sarah Holden, Peter Brady, Michael Hadley, "401(k) Plans: A 25-Year Retrospective," Investment Company Institute, *Research Perspective*, vol. 12, no. 2, (2006).

[10] To calculate 2006 constant dollars, we used consumer price index information for the most current year available from the 2007 Economic Report of the President, p.302.

[11] The 2005 data gathered by the Employee Benefit Research Institute (EBRI)/Investment Company Institute (ICI) joint project represents about 42 percent of estimated 401(k) plan assets, 37 percent of the estimated plan participant universe and about 11 percent of the estimated total number of 401(k) plans. See Sarah Holden and Jack VanDerhei, "401(k) Plan Asset Allocation, Account Balances, and Loan Activity in 2005," Research Perspective, vol. 12, no. 1, (2006) and "Appendix: Additional Figures for the EBRI/ICI Participant- Directed Retirement Plan Data Collection Project for Year-End 2005," Research Perspective, vol. 12, no. 1A, (2006).

[12] A collective investment fund is a trust managed by a bank or trust company that pools investments of retirement plans or other large institutional investors.

[13] The stable value funds typically offered as 401(k) investment options by insurance companies and banks generally provide a guaranteed rate of return over a specific period of time, such as 3 to 5 years.

[14] Balanced funds are pooled accounts invested in both stocks and bonds.

[15] "Private Pension Plan Bulletin Abstract of 2003 Form 5500 Annual Reports," U.S. Department of Labor (Washington, D.C.: Oct. 2006).

[16] Sarah Holden and Jack VanDerhei, "Appendix: Additional Figures for the EBRI/ICIParticipant-Directed Retirement Plan Data Collection Project for Year-End 2005," 10.

[17] Section 404(c) of ERISA generally relieves the fiduciaries of participant-directed plans from liability for any loss or breach that results from a participant's investment decisions about his or her plan assets. 29 U.S.C. § 1104(c) (2000). To be entitled to this relief, the plan must meet the standards promulgated by Labor. 29 C.F.R. § 2550.404c-1 (2006).

[18] AARP Policy Institute, "Pension Participant Knowledge About Plan Fees," *Data Digest* (November 2004).

[19] Mutual funds include their expense ratios in their prospectuses. Other investment options may not provide prospectuses but have expense ratio equivalents that investment industry professionals can identify.

[20] Office of Compliance Inspections and Examinations, *Staff Report Concerning Examinations of Select Pension Consultants,* U.S. Securities and Exchange Commission (Washington, D.C.: May 16, 2005).

[21] *Final Report of the 2004 ERISA Advisory Council Working Group, Health and Welfare Form 5500 Requirements* (Washington, D.C.: Nov. 10, 2004).

[22] 71. Fed. Reg. 41,392 (July 21, 2006).

[23] *Final Report of the 2004 ERISA Advisory Council Working Group, Health and Welfare Form 5500 Requirements* (Washington, D.C.: Nov. 10, 2004).

In: Impact of Financial Crisis on Retirement Security
Editor: John J. Turner
ISBN: 978-1-60692-960-5

Chapter 2

H.R. 3185: THE 401(K) FAIR DISCLOSURE FOR RETIREMENT SECURITY ACT OF 2007 *

John J. Topoleski

SUMMARY

As households become more reliant on 401(k) plans for retirement income, policymakers have become more concerned that participants are unaware of the fees charged in their 401(k) plans. Small differences in fees charged can have large impacts on 401(k) account balances upon retirement. This report provides information on the kinds of fees that are charged in 401(k) plans and details the provisions of H.R. 3185, the 401(k) Fair Disclosure for Retirement Security Act as introduced on July 14, 2007. was passed by the Committee on Education and Labor by a vote of 25-19 on April 16, 2008. It will updated to reflect other 401(k) fee disclosure legislation.

BACKGROUND ON 401(K) FEES

The Structure of 401(k) Plans and the Importance of Fees

Many employers provide defined contribution retirement plans to their employees. In defined contribution plans, employees and/or employers contribute to an individual employee's account, which accrues investment returns. Upon retirement, employees use the accounts as a source of income. Defined contribution plans may be "qualified" if they meet certain Internal Revenue Service (IRS) guidelines with respect to pension plan contributions, benefits, and distributions. 401(k) plans are qualified plans that include a cash or deferred arrangement under which participants can choose to contribute part of their before-tax compensation to the plan rather than receive the compensation in cash. 29 U.S.C. § 402(g)(1)

* This is an edited, reformatted and augmented version of a CRS Report for Congress publication dated April 2008.

allows employees to contribute a pre-tax maximum of $15,500 in 2008 to their individual 401(k) accounts.

Three groups are affected by fees associated with 401(k) plans: (1) plan participants, (2) plan sponsors, and (3) service providers. The plan participants are the employees of the company who have individual accounts to which the employees, the employer, or both contribute. The plan sponsors are the employers. They arrange for service providers to administer the plan. Service providers provide a number of services for plan sponsors and participants including the day-to-day plan business such as recording transactions, arranging for loans, or cashing out retirees' accounts. Service providers may provide all of the services to a plan or may contract out some or all plan services. Prior to choosing a service provider, plan sponsors might ask several providers for details on the products they offer and the fees they charge.

Under the Employee Retirement Income Security Act (ERISA, P.L. 93-406), plan sponsors have a fiduciary responsibility; that is, they must carry out their responsibilities prudently and solely in the interest of the plan's participants.[1] Among other duties, fiduciaries have a responsibility to ensure that the services provided to their plan are necessary and that the cost of those services is reasonable.

There has been a growing interest in the fees that participants in 401(k) plans are charged. Small differences in fees will have large differences in account balances at retirement, especially in the case of yearly or recurring fees.[2] For example, **Table 1** shows the effect that a 0.5%, a 1.0%, and a 1.5% annual fee would have on an initial $20,000 account balance that earns 7% yearly. After 20 years, the account would have about $77,000 if no fee is charged, whereas the account would have about $70,000 if a 0.5% fee is charged. The account would have 17% less (or a balance of about $58,000) if a 1.5% fee is charged. The complexity of 401(k) plan arrangements may provide opportunities for fees to be higher than they otherwise might be, particularly if plan sponsors and participants are not fully informed of the fees they pay. Policies that increase the transparency of fee arrangements may result in participants paying lower fees.

Types of 401(k) Fees

The Employee Benefits Security Administration (EBSA) is an agency within the Department of Labor (DOL). It is charged with protecting the integrity of employee benefits, including retirement plans. An EBSA publication, *A Look At 401(k) Plan Fees*, describes three types of fees.[3]

Table 1. Effect of Annual Fees on a $20,000 Balance (Assuming 7% Annual Return)

	0.0% Annual Fee	0.5% Annual Fee	1.0% Annual Fee	1.5% Annual Fee
Account Balance After 20 years	77,394	70,473	64,143	58,355
Account Balance After 30 years	152,245	132,287	114,870	99,679

Source: CRS calculations.

Plan Administration Fees

These are fees for the day-to-day operations of plans such as record keeping, accounting, legal, and trustee services. Additional services might also be provided, such as access to customer service representatives, educational seminars, or daily valuation. The amount charged for administrative fees can vary depending on the quantity and quality of the services offered. For example, service providers that offer website access with extensive online services might charge higher fees than service providers that provide only basic website services. Administrative fees may be charged either as a flat fee per participant or as a percentage of plan assets.

Investment Fees

According to the EBSA publication, *A Look At 401(k) Plan Fees,* investment-related fees are the largest component of 401(k) plan fees.[4] These cover the costs of transactions within investment options, such as the trades a particular mutual fund makes. Some investment fees include the following:

- **Sales Charges**: These are also known as loads. A front-end load is charged upon investing in some mutual funds. Front-end loads reduce the amount of the initial investment. Back-end loads (also called deferred sales charges or redemption fees) are charged upon selling mutual funds.

- **Rule 12b-1 fees:** These are annual fees that may be charged by mutual funds from fund assets to pay for promotional costs and commissions to brokers and other salespeople. A point of contention is that service providers may receive 12b-1 fees for including particular mutual funds as investment options for participants in the plans they administer.

- **Soft dollar fees:** These payments are for brokerage firm services (such as research) other than commissions for trade execution.

Individual Service Fees

Individuals are charged fees that are associated with using optional features in a 401(k) plan, such as loan origination fees. Fee arrangements may also be "bundled" where some of the services provided or investment alternatives offered to a 401(k) plan may be offered for a single fee. From this single fee, the provider will then pay other providers who have been contracted to provide services to the plan.

Documents Required by Current Law

Current law requires some, but not all, 401(k) fees to be disclosed in three documents: Summary Plan Descriptions (SPDs), Account statements, and Summary Annual Reports.

Summary Plan Descriptions

SPDs describe how plans operate.[5] Plan sponsors are required to automatically provide copies of these documents to plan participants upon enrollment and upon written request of plan participants. Among other items, SPDs contain information about eligibility and vesting requirements, plan benefits, and the source of contributions. Fees paid by third parties to service providers and relationships service providers have with third party providers of services are not required to be disclosed in the SPD.

Annual Report Form 5500

Form 5500 is required to be submitted annually by many ERISA-covered plans. It contains various schedules with information on the financial condition, the investments, and operations of the plans. On November 16, 2007, EBSA issued regulations to require disclosure of fee arrangements on form 5500. The regulation requires plan sponsors to disclose compensation that service providers receive from parties other than plan sponsors, for example, 12b-1 fees.[6]

Benefit Statements

Section 508 of the Pension Protection Act (P.L. 109-280) requires plan sponsors to provide participants in defined contribution plans with quarterly benefit statements if the investments are participant-directed and annual statements if the investments are not participant-directed. The quarterly benefit statement must include the value of each investment in the individual's account, an explanation of any limitations or restrictions on any right of the participant or beneficiary under the plan to direct an investment, and an explanation of the importance of a well-balanced and diversified investment portfolio for long-term retirement security.

H.R. 3185: The 401(k) Fair Disclosure for Retirement Security Act of 2007

Representative George Miller introduced H.R. 3185, the 401(k) Fair Disclosure for Retirement Security Act of 2007 on July 14, 2007. As introduced, this bill would require: (1) service providers to disclose more information on the fees associated with a particular 401(k) plan to plan sponsors and any relationships that service providers have with entities providing services to a 401(k) plan; (2) plan sponsors to inform 401(k) participants about their investment options and the kinds and amounts of fees associated with the investment options; (3) plan sponsors to provide each participant in a 401(k) plan with a detailed breakdown of the fees a participant paid in the previous year; (4) each 401(k) plan to include at least one investment option which is a nationally recognized market-based index fund; and (5) DOL to establish an Advisory Council on Improving Employer-Employee Retirement Practices.

Disclosures from Service Providers to Plan Sponsors

The following provisions in H.R. 3185, as introduced, would require service providers to provide fee information to plan sponsors of 401(k) plans for any contract greater than $1,000.

- H.R. 3185 would require that plan sponsors receive a Service Disclosure Statement from 401(k) plan service providers. The statement would identify who would be performing services under the contract and the costs of such services. In cases where services are bundled or the costs are unknown, H.R. 3185 would require service providers to reasonably allocate costs among the bundled services.
- At a minium, the expected cost of the following services would be identified in the Service Disclosure Statement: commissions for making sales; start-up fees; investment management expenses; estimated trading expenses; administration and record keeping expenses; legal fees; trustee fees; termination charges; total asset based fees; 1 2b- 1 fees; soft dollar commissions; and other costs as specified by the Secretary of Labor.
- H.R. 3185 would require disclosure of any conflicts of interest that a service provider has with the plan sponsor or any third party providing services to the plan for which the service provider receives a payment
- H.R. 3185 would require disclosure of the existence of different share classes within the mutual fund investments offered. For example, mutual funds may offer a number of share classes that offer differing services (with differing fees) or offer share classes that are available only to institutional investors.

Disclosures from Plan Sponsors to Plan Participants

The following are provisions in H.R. 3185 that would require plan sponsors to provide fee information to all plan participants where the participant exercises control over the assets in the account.

- H.R. 3185 would require plan administrators to provide an "Advance Notice of Available Investment Options" to all plan participants on an annual basis. The following information would be required for each investment option: the name of the option; the investment objective; the risk level; whether the option by itself achieves long-term financial security; the historical return; the percentage fee; an explanation of any asset-based fees and/or annual fees; and a comparison to a nationally recognized index or benchmark.
- H.R. 3185 would require a fee menu that would detail the potential service fees that could be assessed against the account in the plan year. The fee menu would have to provide information in relation to the following three categories of fees: (1) fees that vary depending on the investment option selected (e.g., expense ratios or asset-based fees); (2) fees that are assessed as a percentage of total assets in an account; and (3) administration fees that are either automatically deducted each year or that are transaction-based (such as loan origination fees).

- The fee menu would have to describe the purpose of each fee and disclose the extent to which conflicts of interest may exist with respect to service providers or other parties receiving fees.

Annual Benefit Statement to Plan Participants

The following are provisions in H.R. 3185 that would require plan sponsors to provide information to each plan participant regarding the fees paid in his/her account.

- H.R. 3185 would require plan sponsors to provide each plan participant with an annual statement that discloses the following information: the starting and ending balances of the participant's account; the vesting status (e.g. whether the employee is eligible to keep the employer's contributions to the account); the percentage net return for the year; fees assessed for the year; the participant's asset allocation categorized by investment option, including the change in each asset's value during the year and the net return of each asset expressed as both a dollar amount and a percentage; and the service fees charged for each asset investment option, including the underlying investment fees and expense ratios, load fees, asset-based fees, mortality and expense charges, guaranteed investment contract fees, employer stock fees, brokerage charges, plan administration fees, total fees, and total fees as a percentage of current assets. Plan sponsors may provide reasonable estimates of fees in any case where the actual fee is not known.

Minimum Investment Option Requirement

H.R. 3185 would require 401(k) plans to include at least one investment option that is a nationally recognized market-based index fund. The bill does not specify a particular fund, but examples might include mutual funds that replicate the movements of the Dow Jones Industrial Average or Standard & Poor's (S&P) 500 index.

Advisory Council on Improving Employer-Employee Retirement Practices

H.R. 3185 would establish an Advisory Council on Improving Employer-Employee Retirement Practices in DOL. The duties of the Council would include the following:

- The Council would hold hearings, issue advisories on pension plan best practices, present academic and peer-reviewed research regarding pension plan best practices, and maintain a presence on the DOL website.
- The Council would issue an annual report on the state of retirement income security in the United States that includes data on operation of employer-sponsored pensions and recommendations for reform.

End Notes

[1] For more information see CRS Report RL34443, *Summary of the Employee Retirement Income Security Act (ERISA)*, by Patrick Purcell and Jennifer Staman.

[2] For a detailed analysis see CRS Report RL34213, *Retirement Savings Accounts: Fees, Expenses, and Account Balances*, by Patrick Purcell.

[3] Available at [http://www.dol.gov/ebsa/pdf/40 1kFeesEmployee.pdf].

[4] Available at [http://www.dol.gov/ebsa/pdf/40 1kFeesEmployee.pdf].

[5] See 29 CFR § 2920.103-2 and 29 CFR § 2920.103-3 for regulations concerning the style and contents of SPDs.

In: Impact of Financial Crisis on Retirement Security
Editor: John J. Turner
ISBN: 978-1-60692-960-5

Chapter 3

BEHAVIORAL FINANCE, THE MARKET CRISIS AND RETIREMENT SAVINGS

Shlomo Benartzi

Thank you Chairman Miller and members of the House Committee on Education and Labor for the opportunity to share with you my views on behavioral finance, the market crisis and retirement savings.

My name is Shlomo Benartzi. I am a Professor and co-chair of the Behavioral Decision Making Group at the Anderson School of Management at UCLA. I am also co-founder of the Behavioral Finance Forum (BeFi). I have spent the last 15 years researching participant behavior in 401(k) plans, with a particular focus on using behavioral economics to increase retirement savings and retirement security. Some of you might be familiar with the automatic savings increase program Richard Thaler of the University of Chicago and I designed about a decade ago, which we dubbed Save More Tomorrow (or SMarT).

Let me begin my testimony by outlining the behavioral principles that guide retirement savers and how these behavioral tendencies could undermine the retirement security of 401(k) participants in the current environment. To keep this report brief, let me focus on just three behavioral principles that could weaken retirement security.

1. *Buy High, Sell Low:* Individuals have a tendency to buy at the peak, and then panic when markets drop and sell at the bottom. We saw this happen with the Internet bubble when individuals bought a lot of technology stocks at the end of 1999 and the beginning of 2000 right before the market crashed. We also saw individuals pulling money out of the stock market in 2002 right before the market started to go up. There is a real concern that individuals will repeat the same mistake during this market crisis and sell at the bottom and perhaps even stop contributing to their retirement plan.

2. *Myopic Loss Aversion:* The term "myopic loss aversion" refers to the tendency of individuals to focus on short-term losses, even if they have 20 or 30 years until retirement. The myopic focus on short-term losses could result in individuals chasing

safety and placing all their retirement savings in cash. And, we know that a portfolio invested 100 percent in cash is unlikely to provide the long - term growth that many individuals need to fund their retirement. The unusual market volatility we have experienced over the past few weeks and months could magnify the degree of myopia and loss aversion individuals display.

3. *Excessive extrapolation:* Individual investors tend to place too much weight on past performance. For example, many buy stock funds after they see a few years of positive returns. Similarly, the propensity of employees to invest in company stock is highly correlated with the past performance of company stock. I suspect that a lot of employees who were chasing performance and invested heavily in company stock a couple of years ago have recently suffered major losses. This probably includes many employees of financial institutions who invested in company stock and lost their savings and jobs at the same time. Interestingly, preliminary data on recent activity in 401(k) plans indicates that the average participant moved money into company stock in September and early October, probably misjudging the risk of company stock.

The three behavioral principles outlined above highlight the risk of individuals mismanaging their retirement savings, especially in the current economic environment. And, I do believe some retirement savers will panic and bail out of the stock market at the wrong time. I also believe, however, that inertia is extremely powerful and a lot of individuals are likely to procrastinate and never take any action. In the current environment, sticking to one's longterm plans and avoiding impulsive actions might actually be the best decision, even if it is caused by inertia and procrastination.

Having highlighted "behavioral obstacles" that tend to undermine the retirement security of many people, the real question is what can be done to help employees better plan for retirement? I believe Congress has already made significant contributions to the retirement security of Americans with the Pension Protection Act. In particular, automatic enrollment and automatic increases made saving for retirement a lot easier for many Americans. Similarly, clarifying what constitutes a Qualified Default Investment Alternative made plan sponsors more comfortable choosing balanced portfolios on behalf of their plan participants, rather than playing it safe with the most conservative option. However, our system should be improved to help individuals better plan for retirement. Below I list three key areas that I believe could be improved.

1. *Participant Information:*

   a. *Highlight Long-Term Performance on First Page of Statements:* Defined contribution plans are required to provide quarterly statements. Unfortunately, a lot of plan providers interpret that requirement as having to highlight the most recent quarter's performance on the first page of the statement. Since individuals are already obsessed with short-term performance, why not use the quarterly statements as an opportunity to promote long-term thinking? In particular, I propose that the statements display longer-term results on the first page, then provide the recent quarter numbers on the second (or last) page. While this might be permissible under the current law, an endorsement of the idea might be all that is needed to get plan providers to design more sensible participant communications.

b. *Provide Retirement Income Projections on Statements:* I argue that most individuals are ill-equipped to analyze rates of return. The goal of a retirement plan is to provide retirement income, so why not translate account balances, deferral rates and investment elections into projected retirement income? Such projections would not be exact, but they would certainly be more informative for the average plan participant. And, they would dampen the effects of volatile financial markets, as they would incorporate both existing balances and future contributions. For example, someone who just experienced a 40 percent decline in his/her account balance might notice just a 10 percent decline in his projected retirement income once future contributions are taken into account. Again, an endorsement might be all that is needed to get plan providers to add income projections to quarterly statements.

2. *Company Stock:*

a. *Stop the Preferential Treatment of Company Stock:* Company stock enjoys special treatment under ERISA, exempting it from the diversification requirement. It is the only investment option offered to plan participants that is undiversified. I believe, however, that all investments offered to plan participants should be well-diversified, that is, comply with ERISA's diversification requirement. I would like to clarify that I am not proposing to disallow company stock in defined contribution plans. I am just proposing that company stock pass the same fiduciary standards other investments must pass. Of course, if company stock is inherently undiversified and will fail basic fiduciary standards, then plan sponsors will voluntarily stop offering it. I view that as a good thing. We saw thousands of Enron employees lose their jobs and retirement savings simultaneously, and I predict the current crisis will result in many more employees losing their retirement savings due to concentrated positions in company stock.

b. *Endorse Gradual Diversification Programs:* Many plan sponsors are concerned about the financial security of employees investing in company stock. However, they do not know what to do about it. If they tell employees to diversify and sell the stock, then employees might wrongly believe that the company is in trouble. And, if they offer employees the option to gradually trim down their company stock exposure, they could possibly be liable for selling the stock at the wrong time. Professor Richard Thaler and I promote the idea of offering employees the option to gradually sell their stock holdings, perhaps keeping a modest amount of say five percent of their savings in company stock. We dubbed our proposed program, "Sell More Tomorrow." Endorsing some type of a gradual diversification program could make plan sponsors more comfortable addressing the company stock problem before it is too late.

3. *Retirement Income Solutions:*

a. *Define "Qualified Retirement Income Solutions":* The Pension Protection Act has shed light on best practices for the accumulation stage. In particular, it endorsed automatically enrolling employees into retirement savings plans and automatically escalating their deferral rates overtime. We are already seeing that the mere endorsement of these best practices by Congress resulted in many plan sponsors adopting the proposed changes.
Unfortunately, the Pension Protection Act did not spell out best practices for the decumulation phase. In particular, it did not provide any guidance on what would constitute appropriate retirement income solutions for employees getting ready to retire. As a result, the vast majority of plan sponsors are totally confused about: (a) whether or not making retirement income solutions available to retiring employees is part of their duties and responsibilities, and (b) what type of retirement income solutions would be prudent to offer. Given that, it is not surprising that most plan sponsors do not offer any retirement income solution through the plan. Retirees are given a lump sum of cash and sent out into their golden years searching for a solution on their own. As we all know, most individuals are ill - equipped to handle such a complicated financial decision.
I encourage regulators and legislators to shed light on best practices for the decumulation stage. Again, I believe an endorsement would encourage the industry – both plan sponsors and providers – to create and offer competitive retirement income solutions.
The current financial crisis also highlights the need to rethink the type of retirement income solutions that would be prudent. For example, is an immediate annuity that pays monthly income for life prudent, given that insurance companies have recently failed to properly manage risks? I do not necessarily have the answers, but I do know that without guidance from regulators and legislators, plan sponsors will not offer any retirement income solutions. And, I do know that retiring employees are ill - equipped to set a sensible drawdown program on their own, especially in the current volatile environment.

b. *Evaluate Longevity Bonds:* Both defined benefit and defined contribution plans face longevity risk, that is, the risk that people will live much longer than was anticipated, leading to the possibility that plan assets will run out. Note that insurance companies do not presently have the financial instruments available to them to manage systematic increases in longevity where most people end up living longer than reserved for. Systematic longevity risk is simply too large for insurance companies to handle. Furthermore, it is not diversifiable internationally, as medical advances in say the US will end up increasing longevity in all countries sooner or later.

The government could help facilitate the creation of a market for hedging systematic longevity risk by issuing longevity bonds. These are bonds that pay more if people live longer and vice versa, and are similar in concept to TIPS (which allow the private sector hedge another systematic risk, namely inflation risk). Not only would longevity bonds enable retirement plans to better manage longevity risk, they would, more importantly, enable insurance companies to

> better price and guarantee lifetime income streams. This is because longevity bonds would help to establish the market price of longevity risk, in the same way that TIPS help to establish the inflation risk premium. I must admit I am not an expert on launching new markets, but there are experts who have studied these issues extensively. I think establishing a committee to evaluate the merits of longevity bonds is appropriate. Professors David Blake and Robert Shiller would be superb candidates to serve on such a committee.

In summary, improving participant information, addressing the company stock problem and incorporating retirement income solutions into defined contribution plans could enhance the retirement security of millions of people. And, some of the changes I propose could also address behavioral obstacles such as myopic loss aversion and excessive extrapolation.

Keeping in mind the regulatory burden employers already face by offering a retirement plan, my proposals focus on endorsing better practices without necessarily *forcing* or *requiring* plan sponsors and plan providers to implement new or expensive options. To the extent that the proposed changes make sense, I believe mere endorsement by regulators and legislators might be sufficient to make a difference.

Again, thank you Chairman Miller and members of the committee for the opportunity to share my views.

In: Impact of Financial Crisis on Retirement Security
Editor: John J. Turner
ISBN: 978-1-60692-960-5

Chapter 4

RESTORING RETIREMENT SECURITY: THE MARKET CRISIS, THE "GREAT RISK SHIFT", AND THE CHALLENGE FOR OUR NATION

Jacob S. Hacker

Thank you Chairman Miller and members of the House Committee on Education and Labor for the opportunity to share with you my views on the current financial crisis and the future of our nation's embattled framework for providing retirement security.

My name is Jacob Hacker, and I am a professor of political science and co-director of the Center for Health, Economic, and Family Security at the University of California at Berkeley. I have devoted much my career to studying America's distinctive public-private system for providing economic security, including retirement security.

Without mincing words, that retirement security is in peril. Increasingly, Americans find themselves on a shaky financial tightrope, without an adequate safety net if they lose their footing. A major cause of this precariousness is what I call the "great risk shift."[1] Over the last generation, we have witnessed a massive transfer of economic risk from broad structures of insurance, whether sponsored by the corporate sector or by government, onto the fragile balance sheets of American families.

Retirement security is perhaps the clearest example of this shift. A generation ago, if a worker had been offered a retirement plan by his or her employer, it would have been a traditional guaranteed pension that looked much like Social Security. Today, those workers who are lucky enough to receive a pension—and roughly half the workforce continues to lack a pension at their job—are almost universally enrolled in individual account plans like 401(k)s, in which returns are neither predictable nor guaranteed.

The current financial crisis has cast in stark relief the financial market risks that workers face in their 401(k) plans. But market risks are not the only risks transferred to workers by 401(k)s. And fixing 401(k)s will require more than simply encouraging greater savings and more diversified investments. It will require rethinking and rebuilding the private pension system to fit the needs of a transformed American economy.

In my remarks, I would like to review some of the major evidence that Americans planning for retirement are at increased economic risk. After laying out the problem, I call for bold action to restore a measure of shared risk in private retirement planning. My remarks are divided into five parts, each encapsulating a simple core point:

1. Our traditional tripartite framework of retirement security (government, employers, individuals) has broken down as employers have backed away from guaranteed retirement benefits.
2. This breakdown has resulted in a private pension system that works extremely poorly for lower- and middle-income Americans.
3. The main way in which this system works poorly is with regard to protecting Americans against the major risks they face in planning for retirement.
4. Because it takes so long for retirement pension systems to mature, the problems we see in our system today represent only the tip of the iceberg.
5. Restoring a measure of shared risk will require fundamental reform of the 401(k) system, not simply the encouragement of more or smarter investments.

1. America's Distinctive—and Endangered—Retirement Security System

America's framework for providing retirement security was historically referred to as a "three-legged stool": Social Security, private pensions, and personal savings. Each leg was supposed to carry an important part of the weight of securing workers' retirement. For lower-income workers, Social Security was far and away the most important leg of the stool. But for middle- and higher-income workers, tax-favored private pensions were assumed to be vital for achieving a secure retirement—especially after the Employee Retirement Security Act of 1974 put in place rules designed to ensure that defined-benefit pension plans would be properly run, broadly distributed, and secure.

The problem is tnhat this unique employment-based system is coming undone, and in the process risk is shifting back onto workers and their families. As recently as twenty-five years ago, more than 80 percent of large and medium-sized firms offered a defined-benefit plan; today, less than a third do, and the share continues to fall.[2] Companies are rapidly "freezing" their defined-benefit plans (that is, preventing new workers from joining the plan), and shifting them over to alternative forms (such as the so-called cash-balance plan) that are more like 401(k)s. For workers fortunate enough to receive a pension, 401(k) plans have become the default source of private retirement protection.

401(k) plans are not "pensions" as that term has been traditionally understood: a fixed benefit in retirement. They are essentially private investment accounts sponsored by employers. As a result, they greatly increase the degree of risk and responsibility placed on individual workers in retirement planning. Traditional defined-benefit plans are generally mandatory and paid for largely by employers (in lieu of cash wages). They thus represent a form of forced savings. Defined-benefit plans are also insured by the federal government and heavily regulated to protect participants against mismanagement. Perhaps most important, their fixed benefits protect workers against the risk of market downturns and the possibility of living longer than expected (so-called longevity risk).

None of this is true of defined-contribution plans. Participation is voluntary, and many workers choose not to participate or contribute inadequate sums.[3] Plans are not adequately regulated to protect against poor asset allocations or corporate or personal mismanagement. The federal government does not insure defined-contribution plans. And defined-contribution accounts provide no inherent protection against market or longevity risks. Indeed, some features of defined-contribution plans—namely, the ability to borrow against their assets, and the distribution of their accumulated savings as lump- sum payments that must be rolled over into new accounts when workers lose or change jobs—exacerbate the risk that workers will prematurely use retirement savings, leaving inadequate income upon retirement. And, perversely, this risk falls most heavily on younger and less highly paid workers, the very workers most in need of protection.

As private risk protections have eroded, in sum, workers and their families have been forced to bear a greater burden.[4] Rather than enjoying the protections of pension plans that pool risk broadly, Americans are increasingly facing retirement risks on their own. This transformation has at once made retirement savings less equal and more risky.

2. Unequal Retirement

Today, the three-legged stool of retirement security is wobbly for all but the well off. Social Security still provides a guaranteed foundation of retirement security for low- and middle-income workers. But private pensions no longer provide the risk protections they once did, and private retirement savings are virtually nonexistent among less affluent workers.[5]

The incentives for higher-income Americans to save have ballooned with the expansion of tax-favored investment vehicles like 401(k)s. Yet most Americans receive modest benefits from these costly tax breaks. According to a 2000 analysis, "Treasury data show that two-thirds of the existing tax subsidies for retirement saving (including both private pensions and IRAs) accrue to the top 20 percent of the population. Only 12 percent of these tax subsidies accrue to the bottom 60 percent of the population."[6]

These skewed incentives are reflected in 401(k) account balances. It is often claimed that the "average" American has tens of thousands of dollars in a 401(k), but in fact roughly three-quarters of account holders have less than the widely cited average of $60,000. The median among account-holders is less than $20,000.[7] And all these figures include only those who *have* 401(k)s, when only half of workers have access to a defined-contribution pension plan, and only around a third contribute to one. Overall, around 70 percent of defined-contribution pension and IRA assets are held by the richest fifth of Americans.[8]

Even those who do contribute adequately tend to make common investing errors, like putting their money in low-yield bonds, neglecting to rebalance their accounts periodically, and over-investing in their own company's stock. As Professor Bernatzi points out in his testimony, these errors reflect well-understood biases in retirement planning that are deeply ingrained in the human psyche. Studies suggest, for instance, that simply automatically enrolling workers in 401(k)s, rather than requiring that they opt in, doubles initial participation in 401(k) plans, increasing it to nearly 90 percent.[9] Because of how they are subsidized and structured, 401(k)s are almost tailor-made to produce insufficient retirement savings for ordinary workers—and, indeed, this is one reason they are relatively inexpensive for employers to run.

Much ink has been spilled comparing the returns of 401(k)s and old-style pensions (according to a study of returns between 1985 and 2001, defined-benefit pension plans have actually won, earnings returns that exceed those of their upstart competitors by about 1 percent a year).[10] But the central issue for retirement security is not the return, but the risk. Retirement wealth has not only failed to rise for millions of families; it has also grown more risky, as the nation has shifted more of the responsibility for retirement planning from employers and government onto workers and their families.

3. Risky Retirement

The private retirement fortunes of all but today's oldest workers are dependent on the fate of 401(k)s. And this means, in turn, that these private retirement fortunes are dependent on the future of financial markets. As the recent gyrations of the stock market starkly reveal, financial markets provide an inherently risky basis for retirement planning.

To be sure, there is nothing that requires that 401 (k)s be invested in stocks. Workers are free to buy bonds or a conservative mix of stocks and bonds, and indeed a significant share of workers invest their 401(k)s too conservatively for their age (not surprisingly, these tend to be lower-income workers).[11] Still, stocks do deliver a higher overall return. The problem is that this return comes with higher risk, and 401(k)s place all of this higher risk on workers, offering little of the investment guidance and none of the protections against economic loss that are inherent in defined-benefit pensions.

The risks posed by 401(k)s go beyond investment risks to encompass nearly all of the managerial and savings responsibilities imposed on workers. Consider one of the most distinctive features of defined-contribution plans: the ability of workers to take their pension as a "lump sum" (that is, in the form of cash) when they leave an employer. As a means of protecting retirement wealth, this is of considerable benefit to workers who change jobs frequently—but only if they save the money. Unfortunately, "most people who receive [lump sum distributions] do not roll over the funds into qualified accounts," such as IRAs and other 401(k)s—despite the fact that they must pay taxes on all their benefits, as well as a penalty of 10 percent if they are younger than 55.[12]

A clue to the source of this seemingly irrational behavior is provided by research on what affects workers' use of lump sum distributions. Workers who are laid off are 47 percent less likely to roll over their distributions. Workers who move to get a new job are 50 percent less likely. And workers who leave work to care for a family member are 77 percent less likely. "Overall," as one economist concludes, "the evidence suggests that pension assets have been used to buffer economic shocks to the household."[13]

Finally, it is not so easy to turn a retirement account into a lifetime guaranteed income of the sort that Social Security and defined-benefit pensions provide. To protect oneself against this risk requires purchasing an annuity. Yet most people do not use their 401(k) accounts to buy an annuity—in part because of inherent weaknesses of the annuity market, in panrt because their balances are too small to make the transaction worthwhile, and in part because they discount the possibility that they will outlive their assets.

4. The Fallout

The true effects of the 401(k) revolution on income in retirement have yet to be seen. We will only know them with certainty when today's younger workers start retiring. But the signs are already troubling. Among Americans aged 64 to 74 in 2005 (that is, born between 1931 and 1941), nearly a third lost 50 percent or more of their financial wealth between 1992 and 2002—a rate of wealth depletion that will soon leave them confronting a complete exhaustion of their assets, a much-reduced standard of living, or both. The rate of wealth depletion was even higher among those who reported they were in poor health.[14]

At the same time, debt is a rapidly growing among families with heads older than 55. Between 1992 and 2004, the median debt level among older families with debt rose from $14,498 to $32,000 (in 2004 dollars), with the largest percentage increase occurring among the oldest of the aged (75 or over). The share of older families with debt also rose substantially—from 53.8 percent to 60.6 percent—and, again, most the increase was due to the growing problem of indebtedness among the oldest elderly.[15]

These results suggest that while much attention has been paid to the accumulation of assets *for* retirement, far less has been devoted to the issue of how Americans manage their assets *in* retirement. Defined-benefit plans and Social Security ensure that workers receive a relatively stable income as long as they live. There are no such guarantees when it comes to IRAs and 401(k) plans, and every reason to think that many retirees will exhaust their accounts well before they die.[16]

A more complete—and even more worrisome—picture of how risky retirement has become for Americans is provided by the "Retirement Risk Index," a comprehensive measure of retirement security exhaustively prepared by researchers at Boston College and first released in 2006. According to the index, the share of working-age households that are at risk of being financially unprepared for retirement at age sixty-five has jumped from 31 percent in 1983 to more than 43 percent in 2006. Younger Americans, who have borne the brunt of the transformation of retirement protections, are far more likely to be at risk than older Americans. Roughly *half* of those born from the mid-1960s through the early 1970s are at risk of being financially unprepared, compared with around 35 percent of those born in the decade after World War II.[17] The least financially prepared are low- income Americans—in every age group.

5. Restoring Retirement Security

The promise of private pensions at their heyday was a secure retirement income that, when coupled with Social Security, would allow older Americans to spend their retired years in relative comfort. That promise is now in grave doubt. But reforms to our pension system could make private retirement accounts work better as a source of secure retirement income for ordinary workers and their families.

In the context of the financial market crisis and increased private risk-bearing, securing our one guaranteed system of retirement security, Social Security, is all the more essential. But even with a secure Social Security system, today's workers will need other sources of income in retirement. 401(k)s as they are presently constituted are not the solution. Too few workers are offered them, enroll in them, or put adequate sums in them—a reflection of perverse incentives built into their very structure. Instead, we should create a universal 401(k) that is available to all workers, whether or not their employer offers a traditional retirement plan. Employers would be encouraged to match employer contributions to these plans, and indeed government could provide special tax breaks to employers that offered better matches to lower-wage workers.

Since universal 401(k)s would offered to all workers, there would cease to be any problem with lump-sum payments when workers lost or changed jobs. All benefits would remain in the same account throughout a workers' life. As with 401 (k)s today, this money could only be withdrawn before retirement with a steep penalty. Unlike the present system, however, 401 (k)s would be governed by the same rules that now protect traditional pension plans against excessive investment in company stock. Moreover, I believe that the default investment option under 401(k)s should be a low-cost index fund with a mix of stocks and bonds that automatically shifts over time as workers age to limit market risk as workers approach retirement.

After my criticism of 401 (k)s, it may come as surprise that I think Universal 401 (k)s are the best route forward. But the difference between universal 401 (k)s with strong incentives for contributions and the present system are profound. What is more, I would recommend one dramatic additional change that would fundamentally improve 401 (k)s, transforming them into a source of guaranteed retirement income: Under this proposal, 401(k) accounts would be converted into a lifetime guaranteed income at retirement—unless workers specifically requested otherwise and could show they had sufficient assets to weather market risk. These new annuities could be provided by private firms under strict federal rules or directly by the federal government. Interestingly, this proposal is not so different from an idea that was seriously considered by the developers of the Social Security Act in 1935, who argued that the post office should sell low-cost annuities to those who needed them. In essence, universal 401 (k)s along these lines would bring back something close to a guaranteed private pension.

To help workers' plan ahead, moreover, 401(k) balances should be reported to account holders not simply as a cash sum, but also a monthly benefit amount that workers would receive when they retired if they had average life expectancy—just as Social Security benefits are reported.

The reforms that we need should be bold, swift, and guided by a commitment to shared fate. Today, when our fates are often joined more in fear than hope, it is sometimes hard to remember how much we all have in common when it comes to our economic hopes and values. Indeed, we are more linked than ever, because the great risk shift has increasingly reached into the lives of all Americans. What recent market events remind us of is that, in a very real sense, all of us are in this together. Reforms to our embattled framework of retirement security should reflect that.

Again, thank you Chairman Miller and members of the committee for the opportunity to share my views.

End Notes

[1] Jacob S. Hacker, *The Great Risk Shift: The New Economic Insecurity and the Decline of the American Dream*, rev. and exp. ed.m(New York: Oxford University Press, 2008).

[2] John H. Langbein, "Understanding the Death of the Private Pension Plan in the United States," unpublished manuscript, Yale Law School, April 2006.

[3] Alicia H. Munnell and Annika Sundén, "401(k) Plans Are Still Coming Up Short," Center for Retirement Research Issues in Brief Number 43b, Boston College, March 2006, available online at www.bc.edu/ centers/ crr/issues/ib_43b.pdf.

[4] Incidentally, none of these effects was foreseen or intended. When Congress added Section 401(k) to the tax code in 1978 to resolve some longstanding disputes over profit-sharing plans offered by employers, no mention was made of the change, except a brief note in the congressional report on the 1978 legislation indicating that the effects would be "negligible." Joint Committee on Taxation, General Explanation of the Revenue Act of 1978, 95th Congress, Joint Committee Print (1979), 84.

[5] According to a recent analysis of families with earnings between two and six times the federal poverty level ($40,000 to $120,000 for a family of four) and headed by working-age adults, more than half of middle-class families have no net financial assets whatsoever excluding home equity, and nearly four in five middle-class families do not have sufficient non-housing assets to cover three quarters of essential living expenses for even three months should their income disappear. Essential living expenses include food, housing, clothing, transportation, health care, personal care, education, personal insurance and pensions. Jennifer Wheary, Thomas M. Shapiro and Tamara Draut, *By a Thread: The New Experience of America's Middle Class* (New York: Demos, November 2007), available online at http://www.demos.org/pubs/BaT112807.pdf.

[6] Peter Orszag and Jonathan Orszag, "Would Raising IRA Contribution Limits Bolster Retirement Security For Lower– and Middle-income Families or Is There a Better Way?" Center on Budget and Policy Priorities, Washington, D.C., May 2000, available online at www.cbpp.org/4-12-00tax.htm

[7] Employee Benefit Research Institute, "401(k) Plan Asset Allocation: Account Balances, and Loan Activity in 2006," EBRI Issue Brief No. 308 (August 2007, available online at www.ebri.org/briefs/pdf/EBRI_IB_08-20073.pdf.

[8] Peter Orszag, "Progressivity and Savings: Fixing the Nation's Upside-Down Incentives for Savings," Testimony before the House Committee on Education and the Workforce February 25, 2004, available online at http://www.brookings.edu/views/testimony/orszag/20040225.pdf.

[9] Brigitte C. Madrian and Dennis F. Shea, "The Power of Suggestion: Inertia in 401(k) Participation and Savings Behavior," *The Quarterly Journal of Economics,* Vol. 116, No. 4 (2006), 1159.

[10] Alicia H. Munnell and Annika Sunden, *Coming Up Short: The Challenge of 401(k) Plans* (Washington, D.C.: The Brookings Institution, 2004), 75-77.

[11] Munnell and Sunden, *Coming Up Short,* chap. 4.

[12] Leonard E. Burman, Norma B. Coe, William G. Gale, "What Happens When You Show Them the Money: Lump Sum Distributions, Retirement Income Security and Public Policy," Prepared for Second Annual Joint Conference for the Retirement Research Consortium (2000), available online at http://www.bc.edu/ centers/ crr/papers/SV-2%20Burman%20Coe%20Gale.pdf.

[13] Gary Engelhardt, "Reasons for Job Change and the Disposition of Pre-Retirement Lump Sum Pension Distributions," Unpublished, available online at http://wwwcpr. maxwell.syr.edu/ faculty/ engelhardt/ econ letters.pdf.

[14] Craig Copeland, "Changes in Wealth for Americans Reaching or Just Past Normal Retirement Age," Employee Benefits Research Institute Issue Brief No. 277 (2005), 18.

[15] Employee Benefit Research Institute (EBRI), *Debt of the Elderly and Near Elderly, 1992-2004* (Washington, D.C.: EBRI, September 2006), available online at www.ebri.org/pdf/notespdf/EBRI_Notes_09-20061.pdf.

[16] Jeffrey R. Brown, "How Should We Insure Longevity Risk in Pensions and Social Security," Center for Retirement Research, An Issue in Brief 4 (August 2000), available online at http://www.bc.edu/ centers/ crr/issues/ib_4.pdf.

[17] Alicia H. Munnell, Francesca Golub-Sass, and Anthony Webb, *What Moves the National Retirement Risk Index? A Look Back and An Update* (Boston: Boston College Center for Retirement Research, January 2007), available online at http://crr.bc.edu/images/stories/Briefs/ib_57a.pdf.

In: Impact of Financial Crisis on Retirement Security
Editor: John J. Turner
ISBN: 978-1-60692-960-5

Chapter 5

"THE IMPACT OF THE FINANCIAL CRISIS ON WORKERS' RETIREMENT SECURITY"

Mark A. Davis

Good morning Mr. Chairman and members of the Committee. Thank you for the opportunity to speak with you today. My name is Mark A. Davis and I am a principal in Kravitz Davis Sansone, Inc. a registered investment advisor that is part of the Kravitz organization. Kravitz is the largest independent pension design, consulting and management firm headquartered in California. All we do is service qualified plans, their sponsors and participants. Kravitz administers more than 1,000 plans, mostly of smaller employers, and we serve as fiduciary advisor or investment manager on more than 180 plans of all sizes. We also have a team that spends a great deal of time providing employee meeting and investment education services primarily to smaller companies. I am an independent investment advisor, and in that capacity I do not receive any compensation without the contractual approval of plan sponsors—in most cases I am paid by the plan sponsor or the plan at the direction of the sponsor.

I want to start by adding my voice to those that have expressed appreciation to the hard work done by this Committee on retirement security issues, particularly in regards to fee disclosure. As we sit here today in the third week of a new calendar quarter, American workers are beginning to receive their retirement plan statements for the period ending September 30. It is unfortunate that millions of those plan participants will be receiving statements that do not disclose the fees that they are being charged. It is all the more disturbing in the current performance environment—participants pay those same hidden fees regardless of market losses. The sunshine of better disclosure is badly needed—and thank you for your continued efforts.

The private retirement system, flaws and all, has been a huge success in helping Americans build real wealth for retirement and to pass that wealth on to future generations. This includes not just 401(k) plans but also 403(b) and 457 plans as well that are used in the public sector. Every day we see Americans who are benefiting from the savings discipline that these plans impose. Even with the market turmoil my team tells me that for every person raising concerns about their balances there are many others vocal in their determination to stay with the program in order to maximize their long-term opportunities to build their retirement nest-eggs. On Friday of last week I met with three different groups of employees at a manufacturing firm in Texas. The first two meetings were for shift workers, one group coming on and one group going off, most of whom spoke Spanish as their primary language. While clearly concerned with the economy, these men were unified in their enthusiasm for their 401(k) plan and the Profit Sharing contributions their employer provides. I have served this Plan since 2000 and I have come to have a warm relationship with many of these gentlemen, despite the language and cultural divide that separates us. They now have the experience to know that we got through the last downturn and we will get through this one too. For these workers the plan is a highly valuable means of saving for retirement and of sharing in the success of their company. For many it is their first and only means of saving and building a stake in the system.

It is exciting to note how different the services participants have available to them during this downturn are. When the last bubble burst and the market fell from 2000 to 2002 we did not have as many tools to help as we do now. Very few plans had the chance to use diversified tools like target maturity funds. Automatic enrollment and Qualified Default Investment Alternative protocols were not yet prevalent. Advice and managed account tools had very little market penetration. During those years people in my profession did the hard work of comforting and educating employees, encouraging them to "stay the course" and keep contributing, assuring them that some day the market would actually go up again. Those participants saw significant and real gains during the bull market run from 2003 through 2007. While this recovery, whenever it comes, won't happen in the same way or on the same timeline, long term it will have the same effect.

Let me give you some more examples of what we are seeing and experiencing today. My associates and I have met or communicated by phone or email with scores of participants in the past few weeks.

You have heard statistics concerning the increase in applications for loans as well as hardship and other in-service distributions. Our team that processes loans and withdrawals for the clients we serve, who are again, primarily small businesses, has seen a moderate increase in the number of loans requested over the last year and a significant increase in requests for hardship withdrawals during that same period.

Last week a company whose education services are provided by a large financial institution received a call from an irate participant accusing them of having "taken $10,000 out of his account". My client explained that the drop was due to market losses and made it clear that the participant was not experiencing anything that was unique to him. This participant simply did not understand that the value of his retirement account could go down.

A 52 year old employee of a Texas retailer told me he couldn't stand the volatility in his plan anymore and he wanted to take what was left of his money out to "pay off his house" so his family would have somewhere to live when he got fired. I did the best I could to give him the pro's and con's of such a move, but in the end he was determined to find a way to get at the money even though he would have to pay a 10 percent penalty tax on top of income tax.

I spent time on the phone with an attorney who was irate that his ability to trade his account had been limited by his financial institution vendor, a practice put in place in 2004 in response to regulatory pressures stemming from the mutual fund trading scandals earlier this decade.

There are times when the business of conducting employee education meetings is truly rewarding. Helping people to understand and maximize their opportunities for retirement savings success is a mission for many of us in the field. For most working Americans, the closest they will ever get to professional investment advice are the encounters they have with investment educators, either independents, like us, or employees of their primary retirement services vendors. There are also times when it can be very challenging counseling participants, particularly older ones, who have experienced sometimes significant investment losses. But make no mistake. Investment sophistication has no correlation to the color of the collar. Many blue-collar Americans are no more at sea than many of their white-collar counterparts. There is a huge need to educate all Americans, from their early years, on the basics of financial education, from retirement savings to mortgage rates. That education cannot be left to the private sector.

Automatic enrollment has also spawned a new and potentially culture changing waive of co-opted participation among employee and people groups that have been unintentionally "carved out" by prior positive enrollment protocols. Unfortunately many of these new automatic enrollment programs have just been put in place in this year. The result is that many first time participants have been brought into the system and invested in diversified portfolios, most frequently age based target maturity funds, and have experienced unprecedented downdrafts in the last few months. Some of these people feel distraught and some even betrayed. Our challenge now is to keep those people engaged and committed long enough for them to benefit from the long term return of market stability and success. More education is called for.

Plan sponsors are faced with unique challenges that are evolving even as we sit here today. The recent volatility has forced several plans we serve to put much needed changes on hold as Human Resources staffs have balked at making changes that might scare employees. Making plan level investment menu changes has also been made much more difficult and needlessly complex by the inconsistent enforcement of short-term redemption fee policies resulting from the trading scandals earlier this decade. Every mutual fund company and financial institution has its own rules and they are not enforced consistently. Both sponsors and participants are intimidated and confused by the inconsistencies.

Many plan sponsors, particularly in the small plan area of the marketplace, use annuity products from insurance companies as the vehicle for their retirement plans. These products generally offer a broad array of investment choices, managed by multiple, diverse investment managers, from which the sponsor can select an investment menu to offer participants. They have evolved greatly over the years and when used properly can offer an excellent means for providing a retirement benefit program. Often, though, they come with a "catch". The only alternative some of these products make available for the most risk averse participants are quote "guaranteed" accounts. In many if not most cases we have seen these consist of investments in the General Accounts of the sponsoring insurance company. Many times a plan sponsor or participant's ability to withdraw from these accounts is severely constrained in return for the perceived value of the "guarantee". It is our understanding that, in the event of a failure of an insurer, these accounts would have only marginal preference over other creditors in the event of insolvency of the insurer.

We have seen plans with 60-70% of their assets invested in such vehicles. While on an absolute return basis they may look good this year, no one would argue that investing 60-70% of a plan's assets in a bond of that one insurer, or the stock of that one insurer, or any one company for that matter, would be prudent. Yet that is exactly what many plans are doing. We know from brutal experience that most participants who use these investments have no idea of the risks to which they are truly exposed. They believe the word "guarantee". In these days of volatility, much money is pouring in to these accounts at the exact time that many insurers are under the most extreme pressure. It is critically important that just as participants need to diversify their investments, plan sponsors need to offer diversified investment choices. As far as I know, the Department of Labor has not focused on this.

If I may I would like to take a moment to offer you my thoughts regarding the current status of investment education in the retirement system. When I began my career in 1991, I joined the "Employee Communications" department of a major financial services firm. Within a year the department's name, and function, was radically changed. Over night we became the "Investment Education" department as that became a sales differentiator in the marketplace. Our new function was to teach people how to use the investments that we offered, under the name and restrictions of "guidance" not "investment advice". Throughout the decade of the 1990's, as defined benefit plans gave way to defined contribution plans as a society we shifted the burden for retirement funding and investing from sponsors to participants. We did so without any corresponding emphasis on education. We relied on the private sector to provide educational services. The private sector cannot be blamed for doing what is in its own best interests, creating better future clients for itself. It is not in the financial interest of most vendors to spend much time educating the great bulk of American participants, most of whom will never be future clients for most of those firms.

We have seen this all too clearly with several clients. One client, whose business involves a large number of non-highly compensated employees who do physical labor, has a high percentage of employees for whom English is not their primary language. Our client offers a very generous employee matching contribution which very few of their non-highly compensated employees were taking good advantage of. When the client changed vendors and added an automatic enrollment protocol, they met with participants in one on one sessions in the language of their choice, and were able to get employees to truly embrace the program. In retrospect many of the employees had not really understood the plan and felt it wasn't for them. The pictures and images in all of the enrollment materials used by their prior vendor depicted employees and smiling retirees who were not culturally representative of the broader range of our client's employees.

The plan looked and felt like a benefit for management even though it really is an excellent benefit for all employees.

I want to strongly encourage future efforts at cooperation between the Departments of Labor and Education. If Americans are to be given the responsibility to manage their own retirement investments as a means of lessening the liability of both employers and society, then students from Kindergarten through 12th grade should be taught basic financial principles as a means of getting ready. We still teach Trigonometry, but most Americans graduate high school without knowing the importance of savings, or how credit cards, car loans, and mortgages work. Proper long term education, across cultural lines, will make future generations of Americans hungry for and prepared to handle the retirement plans their future employers will offer.

The current volatility, and the damage it has done, cannot be undone in the near term. Steps like a temporary repeal of minimum required distribution rules may help to alleviate some of the worst pain. You may also want to consider temporarily encouraging all plans to offer hardship withdrawal provisions to prevent foreclosure and eviction. Other steps that encourage more diversified stable value investing and discourage the use of general account products for ERISA assets will also help. If this Committee can help to clarify and make more consistent the rules that govern short term redemption fees and transaction limitations that will remove a major cause of unnecessary plan complexity. Most importantly if you can charge the Departments of Labor and Education to work together to better educate future American workers some of the anxiety and panic being experienced today may be avoided in response to future market turmoil.

Thank you for your time. I will be pleased to answer any questions that I can.

In: Impact of Financial Crisis on Retirement Security
Editor: John J. Turner
ISBN: 978-1-60692-960-5

Chapter 6

"THE IMPACT OF THE FINANCIAL CRISIS ON WORKERS' RETIREMENT SECURITY"

Steve Carroll

Thank you Chairman Miller and Congresswoman Woolsey for providing this hearing. It is reassuring to me that you are determined to develop legislative relief to all of us citizens who have trusted our institutions -- who have operated strictly within the rules government and financial institutions set for us -- and who now find our much anticipated "golden years" rapidly morphing into years of ash and tears -- all through no fault or misdeeds of our own. My story is straightforward and will be short.

In 1972 Chuck Maisel, who is here today, and I formed a partnership as expository writers. Although we have written in myriad formats our specialty grew to become the verbal content of educational exhibits and museums. In short we planned the visitors' experience for each project. Over the years we bought home offices together and developed a mutually satisfactory long-range economic security plan: We paid cash for everything where possible including our home and vehicles. We strictly avoided credit-card interest fees by paying each account in full each month. We selected Kaiser Health Plan for wholly reliable health insurance coverage for life for both of us. And we invested earned income in IRA's since 1974. Financial advisors urged us to put our IRAs in mutual stock funds. We followed that advice but have been under-whelmed by the mutual funds performance/risk ratio.

Just before retirement, in 2005 we sold our mortgage-free home of many years for a very good profit and we purchased a smaller, much less expensive home. Being quite conservative in money management, we declined advice from two financial advisors who urged us to buy stock. We didn't want to gamble security for riches so we placed the remaining profits wholly in AA and AAA rated bonds. The bonds are "laddered" to reach maturity regularly at various times. Additionally, we contracted a forty-year, 6.5% mortgage on our retirement home – from which we planed to be carried out in a hearse and a scholarship we have funded at Sonoma State University would inherit both the house and the our residual investment. The home loan is secured by our retirement investments. With careful budgeting, we could live on the interest of our prudently purchased bonds through our "golden years. At the time we developed this plan, we were told that, in case of the bankruptcy of any of the bond issuers, we would receive reimbursements for our bonds from the remaining assets before stockholders– and our bonds had AA and AAA ratings.

In the interim Chuck turned 70 in 1997, so he had to begin selling his IRA stock. I will reach 70 in 2011. At this time we have the option of converting the IRAs into money market funds, but the net loss would be horrendous and he would have to pay taxes on the amount of sale. Working in concert with our financial advisor, we decided to leave the IRAs as they were until the stock market rose again. In the interim, we would coast nicely on the interest from our bonds. On Monday, September 22nd our investment broker at Morgan Stanley called to advise us that if we sold our Washington Mutual (WaMu) bonds we would lose 45% of our investment. But, in light of the US Treasury's recent history, WaMu would be shored up like Bear Stearns, AIG, Freddy and Fannie. If we held on to our bonds, the worst that could happen was that WaMu would declare bankruptcy, in which case we, as "bondholders" would be reimbursed after first tier debt holders were compensated. We "prudently" hunkered down.

Wham! The FDIC seized WaMu, sold its ***assets*** of over $300 billion including, I suppose, our $100,000 and left us with nothing after the assets were sucked out of WaMu. FDIC then sold those assets to JP Morgan Chase for $1.9 billion. What a deal for Morgan Chase!! We bondholders are left with zero, and who knows who will get the $1.9 billion? As the "thin cats" at J.P. Morgan trot down the road with our money, we seem to be left empty-handed thanks to the FDIC's precipitate action.

Chuck and I, like millions of other citizens, face ugly circumstances for our future. We hope we still will receive interest payments from our other bonds – unless FDIC pulls another midnight raid. But even so, our monthly budget has been severely depleted for life. We still have our IRAs. But, as they are in mutual stock funds they are so far down in value that selling any of them right now, as the law requires of Chuck, the loss is an enormous percentage of the investment -– and then he will be taxed on the total income from the sale to boot! We urge you to develop relief from the sell-and tax rules that destroy the security IRAs were to create.

Finally, of course, we hope that WaMu bondholders can recoup some of our losses in future market relief legislation so that our home, which was bought by the rules and with great prudence, does not end up on this depressed market competing with those of sub-prime borrowers and speculative flippers while we search for living space under an overpass.

Thank you for hearing my remarks. I will answer any questions I can.

In: Impact of Financial Crisis on Retirement Security
Editor: John J. Turner
ISBN: 978-1-60692-960-5

Chapter 7

LESSONS FROM THE FINANCIAL CRISIS FOR RETIREMENT SECURITY: BUILDING BETTER RETIREMENT PLANS, TESTIMONY BEFORE THE U.S. HOUSE OF REPRESENTATIVES COMMITTEE ON EDUCATION AND LABOR, " THE IMPACT OF THE FINANCIAL CRISIS ON WORKERS' RETIREMENT SECURITY," OCTOBER 7, 2008

Christian E. Weller

Thank you Chairman Miller, Ranking Member McKeon, and members of the House Committee on Education and Labor for this opportunity to speak to you today.

My name is Christian Weller. I am an associate professor of public policy in the McCormack Graduate School at the University of Massachusetts Boston, a Senior Fellow at the Center for American Progress Action Fund in Washington, D.C., and an Institute Fellow at the Gerontology Institute at the University of Massachusetts Boston. As my affiliations show, I have substantial expertise and experience working on retirement security issues both in a research and policy context.

I. INTRODUCTION AND OVERVIEW

In my testimony today, I would like to focus on the lessons that can be learned from the current financial crisis for retirement income security. In particular, the long-term trend in declining retirement security has been exacerbated by the recent turmoil in the financial markets, and thus ever more poignantly underscores the need for swift and broad action to vastly improve the retirement income security for the majority of American families. Too many Americans rely too heavily on their homes as their primary source of household wealth. Declines in house prices quickly decimate this wealth, especially when families are heavily leveraged, as has been increasingly the case in the past few years, when mortgages grew faster than home values. And, even those families who have some retirement savings—about three quarters of American families nearing retirement—increasingly rely on their own luck and investment savvy to reach their retirement savings goals. Yet economists have long known that the success of "Do It Yourself" savings plans is severely hampered by the underlying investor psychology, which often leads individual investors to buy and sell low in crises like these.

These data point toward three policy goals. First and foremost, more Americans need retirement savings in addition to Social Security and outside of their own home. Second, Americans need to save more for retirement, encouraged by progressive saving incentives and supported by their employers. Substantially raising Americans' retirement security is a heavily lift, as the data further below show, and thus can only be accomplished as a shared responsibility between individuals, employers, and the public. Third, Americans need to be reassured that the money that they will save for retirement will actually be there when they need it. The exposure to large market swings, as we have experienced twice in the past decade, can send individual investors scrambling for an exit at the most inopportune time. This prevents them from saving enough, and actually increases their exposure to financial market risks.

The policy response to these challenges has to be comprehensive, consistent, and progressive. It needs to be comprehensive because the challenge is large. That is, all well-designed options need to be considered and implemented. No one single silver bullet will accomplish all that needs to get done.[1] Moreover, the policy responses need to be consistent with each other. It is an inconsistent policy approach to try to introduce beneficial features from traditional defined benefit, or DB plans, into 401(k)-style defined contribution, or DC plans, while at the same time pursuing policy approaches that are harmful to the same DB plans that are used as model for retirement savings. And finally, the policy approach needs to be progressive in order to focus especially on those families who are most in need of building retirement wealth and who are currently receiving a disproportionately small share of the existing retirement saving incentives that the public allocates each year for this purpose.

With this in mind, there are several specific policy directions that should be explored. Congress should consider both strengthening existing DB plans and vastly improving existing 401(k)-style defined contribution plans.

On improving DB plans, the financial market swings over the past 10 years have clearly shown that legislative and regulatory efforts should increase the incentives for employers to make regular contributions to their pension plans. A large part of the current crisis in retirement security is that employers often either could not or did not want to make additional contributions to their pension plans. Thus, they may have been less well prepared for the financial market crisis that hit after 2000 and again in 2008. New legislation, particularly the Pension Protection Act of 2006, and proposed accounting rule changes—the same ones that banks are now asking Congress to suspend—require smaller contributions during good economic times and larger employer contributions during bad economic times than past accounting rules did or alternative rules would require.

As for DC plans, there are two separate directions that should be pursued by policymakers to "build a better 401(k)." First, the movement to making saving for retirement simpler needs to be elevated. This would reduce the chance that individual investors will fall prey to the well-known pitfalls of saving for retirement on one's own: reducing contributions when prices drop, not regularly diversifying even when prices change dramatically, buying high and selling low by following fads, and hanging on to too much employer stock, among others. Second, Congress should end the system of "upside-down" saving incentives, whereby those who are least in need of support to save more receive the largest relative incentives, and those who need the most help receive the least public support.

II. It Was Already Bad before the Crisis Hit

While the events that have taken place over the past several weeks have shone a spotlight on how affected Americans' retirement plans can be by such volatility in the financial markets, it is important to keep in mind that Americans' retirement security has been in distress for much longer than the past few weeks. In fact, retirement security has been a growing concern for Americans for many years due to limited retirement plan coverage, little retirement wealth, and increasing risk exposure of the individual.

Too few people are covered by a retirement savings plan at work. In 2007, the most recent year for which data are available, 52.0 percent of full-time private-sector wage and salary workers participated in an employer-sponsored retirement plan. That is more than five percentage points lower than the 57.4 percent who participated in an employer-sponsored plan in 2000. Twenty- three percent of part-time workers participated in such a plan in 2007, down from 26.9 percent in 2000. Thus, overall, just 45.1 percent of all private-sector wage and salary workers participated in an employer-sponsored retirement plan in 2007, down from slightly more than half of all workers—50.3 percent—in 2000. That is, even at its last peak, almost half of all workers did not participate in an employer-sponsored retirement plan and this share has substantially shrunk since then (Purcell, 2008a).[2]

A breakdown by demographics shows that there is little difference in coverage trends by gender. Rates of participation in an employer-sponsored retirement plan have fallen for both men and women since the beginning of the century. In 2007, 51.1 percent of male private-sector wage and salary workers participated in an employer-sponsored plan, well below the 58.3 percent who participated in one in 2000. Women's participation rates have not fallen as far as men's have, but they were not as high as men's rates in 2000 to begin with. In 2000, 56.1 percent of full-time female workers participated in an employer-sponsored retirement plan, but that share shrank to 52.6 percent in 2007 (Purcell, 2008a).

There are, however, substantial differences in retirement saving coverage by race and ethnicity. Minorities are less likely to participate in an employee-sponsored retirement plan than whites, and are also more likely to lack sufficient funds for a secure retirement than their counterparts. In 2002, the first year for which consistent retirement coverage data by race and ethnicity are available from the Bureau of Labor Statistics' Current Population Survey, 58.8 percent of white, non-Hispanic, private-sector wage and salary workers participated in an employer-sponsored retirement plan. Less than half of black, non-Hispanic workers—47.5 percent —and less than one-third—31.1 percent—of Hispanic workers did. Participation rates were lower for all three of these groups of workers in 2007, with 57.6 percent of white workers, 47.1 percent of black, non- Hispanic workers, and only 30.6 percent of Hispanic workers participating in such a plan (Purcell, 2008a).

In addition, participation in retirement saving plans varies with income, such that lower-income workers are markedly less likely than higher-income workers to participate. Participation in employer-sponsored retirement plans has declined for all quartiles of private-sector workers from 2000 to 2007. Importantly, private-sector workers in the bottom half of the wage distribution had especially low participation rates to begin with. In 2000, 55.5 percent of private-sector workers in the third-highest earnings quartile participated in an employer-sponsored retirement plan, but in 2007, less than half—49.7 percent—did. Workers with earnings in the lowest quartile, or less than $27,000, have fared even worse. Less than one-third participated in an employer-sponsored retirement plan in both 2000 and 2007, with rates of 32.1 percent and 27.7 percent, respectively. Even workers in the highest two earnings quartiles have seen their participation rates decline over this period. Slightly more than two-thirds—67.1 percent—of workers in the second-highest income quartile participated in an employer-sponsored plan in 2000, but that share had dropped to 62.8 percent in 2007. Additionally, 69.2 percent of workers in the highest earnings quartile participated in an employer-sponsored retirement plan in 2007, down from roughly threequarters—75.5 percent—in 2000 (Purcell, 2008b).

Much of the low coverage rate for lower-income earners is explained by their personal characteristics. For instance, the Investment Company Institute (Brady and Sigrist, 2008) recently concluded that "most workers who have the ability to save and to be focused primarily on saving for retirement are covered by an employer-provided retirement plan." Low participation is thus often a function of low earnings, young age, and working for a small employer. The link between retirement saving participation and income is also supported by the fact that the gap between being offered a retirement plan at work and participating in such a plan in the private sector is largest for low-income earners (Purcell, 2008a).

Additionally, employer size matters. Brady and Sigrist (2008) conclude that only 18 percent of employees at small businesses—those with less than 10 employees—have access to an employer-sponsored retirement plan, as compared to 71 percent of employees working for an employer with more than 1,000 employees in 2004, based on data from the Federal Reserve's Survey of Consumer Finances. Similarly, Purcell (2008a) finds, based on the Bureau of Labor Statistics' Current Population Survey, that only 29.3 percent of employees working for an employer with fewer than 25 employees had access to an employer-sponsored retirement plan. Additionally, only 25.5 percent of all employees at such businesses participated in such a plan in 2007. In comparison, 75.2 percent of employees at large firms, with more than 100 employees, had access to a plan and 65.4 percent participated in 2007.

The data thus lead to two important conclusions. First, there are substantial differences by demographic characteristics. Second, targeting lower-income workers and small businesses in terms of retirement saving policies may generate the largest dividends in terms of improving retirement wealth generation.

III. THE CRISIS: WEALTH DESTRUCTION IN ACTION

Aggregate data show that household wealth has declined sharply over the past year and thus has taken a serious toll on the retirement security of individuals. With respect to retirement security, it is important to consider total wealth relative to disposable income. For one, wealth is interchangeable. Families, for instance, borrow from their 401(k) plans to pay for their home when they are tapped out on other loans and do not have sufficient savings for the necessary down payment or renovations (Weller and Wenger, 2008). Also, total wealth is a store of future income that can be used to replace income, for instance, in the case of an economic emergency, a disability, a death of a breadwinner, and in retirement.

The trends in total household wealth show that families have lost wealth at a breathtaking speed over the past year. Total real wealth fell by $4.5 trillion dollars from September 2007—the last peak in household wealth—to June 2008. This is an annualized average loss of 10.2 percent for the past three quarters. In comparison, during the first three quarters of the downturn in the early 2000s, from March 2000 to December 2000, the rate of decline averaged to an annualized 6.8 percent. For the entire wealth loss streak from March 2000 to September 2002, it averaged to 7.1 percent. That is, the current wealth loss is more than 40 percent faster than during the last period of wealth loss.[3]

Importantly, this sharp drop in household wealth came after families had not recovered from their relative wealth losses incurred during the last crisis. At its peak, total family wealth amounted to 619.4 percent of disposable income in December 1999. By September 2002, this ratio had fallen to 483.8 percent, before climbing to 575.0 percent in June 2007. For the next four quarters, wealth did not keep pace with disposable income and dropped to 517.4 percent. In other words, if total household wealth had kept pace with disposable income after September 1999, families in June 2008 would have had an additional $11 trillion.[4]

Much of the drop in housing wealth is a consequence of the bursting housing bubble, although an even larger share of total wealth losses is concentrated in financial wealth. Over the three quarters from September 2007 to June 2008, households lost a total of $1.1 trillion in real housing wealth, $351 billion in the last quarter alone. Additionally, their home equity shrank by $1.0 trillion, reflecting a decrease at an annualized average rate of 17.8 percent during those quarters. This was the second-highest drop in real home equity over a three-quarter period and the largest since the first three quarters of 1974. As a result, home equity amounted to 81.2 percent of disposable income in June 2008—its lowest level since the end of 1 976.[5]

The figures clearly show a few noteworthy points. First, the loss in household wealth goes well beyond the recent drop in house prices. Second, the drop in household wealth, especially in real estate wealth, is very sharp. Third, the loss of household wealth has put many families in a precarious financial situation by adding to existing economic woes, such as a weak labor market.

IV. Amid the Crisis, the Public is Worried about Retirement Security

Given growing discomfort, to say the least, in today's economic climate, it should not be surprising that public opinion polling data also indicate that Americans have become increasingly worried about their ability to afford a comfortable retirement. Gallup has polled (non-retiree) Americans about whether they expect to have enough money to live comfortably in retirement. The share of respondents who said that they did expect to have enough money to live comfortably in retirement held steady at 59 percent from 2002 though 2004, before falling to 53 percent in 2005, and dropping to 46 percent in April 2008. The April 2008 Gallup poll also found that nearly two-thirds—63 percent—of Americans are worried that they will not have enough money for their retirement. This share is higher than both the share of Americans who were worried about their ability to pay medical costs associated with an accident or serious illness (56 percent) and the share who were afraid that they will not be able to maintain their current standard of living amid 2008's economic troubles (55 percent) (Jacobe, 2008b).

According to a January 2006 Pew Research Center poll, 71 percent of Americans were either very or somewhat concerned about not having enough money for retirement, up from 60 percent in 2005. This was slightly higher than the 68 percent concerned about their ability to afford necessary health care for their family, and considerably higher than the 44 percent who were concerned about receiving a pay cut or losing their job. An April 2007 Gallup poll found that 56 percent of those surveyed were either very or moderately worried about not having enough money for their retirement. This was a higher percentage than any other economic worry Gallup asked about, including covering unexpected medical costs, maintaining their current standard of living, and paying for housing costs. Especially telling is the fact that even a majority of those in households earning $75,000 or more per year—who would be considered upper-middle income to wealth—indicated that they were worried about their retirement income (Teixeira, 2008).

Other surveys found similar trends. The 2008 Retirement Confidence Survey, which is conducted annually by the Employee Benefit Research Institute, found that both workers' and retirees' retirement security confidence has dropped in recent years. In 2008, just under one-third —61 percent—of workers polled indicated that they were either very confident or somewhat confident in their ability to afford a comfortable retirement, down from 65 percent in 2005. Additionally, current retirees' confidence has declined, with 64 percent indicating that they were very or somewhat confident in their ability to afford a comfortable retirement, down from 80 percent in 2005 (Employee Benefit Research Institute, 2008).

A recent poll conducted by Bankrate Inc. found that only about 3 in 10 workers expected to have enough money to retire comfortably. Nearly 7 in 10 Americans have set low expectations about their retirement prospects. One in five Americans said they were afraid they would never be able to retire (*Austin Business Journal*, 2008).

Another way to see this increased worry about personal retirement security is to examine the change in how workers expect to fund their retirement. For example, in April 2001, only 10 percent of respondents to a Gallup poll expected to use part-time work as a major source of their retirement funding. By April 2005 that share had risen to 18 percent. By April 2008, it had increased even more, to 20 percent (Jacobe, 2008a).

Additionally, many Americans of retirement age are already struggling to make ends meet. In 2007, the median income of Americans ages 65 and older was $17,382. However, their actual incomes varied widely. Importantly, in 2007, one-fourth of people ages 65 and older had incomes of less than $10,722. When one considers just the quickly rising costs of necessities, it is easy to see why Americans, both of retirement age and younger, are concerned about their retirement security. While 57 percent of households with a head of the house or spouse aged 65 or older earned income on assets in 2007, half of them received less than $1,585. The overall mean income from assets among these households was just $2,254 (Purcell, 2008a).

Because of these worries, retirement has remained an important issue on Americans' minds throughout the election year of 2008. A March-April 2008 CBS News/*New York Times* poll showed that while paying everyday bills was the public's top personal economic concern, saving for retirement was the second biggest concern (American Enterprise Institute Public Opinion Studies, 2008). Additionally, an August 2008 poll for George Washington University found that the public viewed retirement as a more important issue for Congress than the mortgage crisis, taxes, or education (Lake Research Partners and The Tarrance Group, 2008).

Clearly there is both public desire for and a defined need to improve the retirement security of America's workers. Policymakers must catch up to fill these voids and design a more fulfilling retirement plan for America's workers. To improve retirement security, we must build a better DC plan and strengthen existing DB plans.

V. Building Better Retirement Plans

If one were to design an ideal retirement plan, it would likely encompass the following features:

- Broad-based coverage, which covers all workers automatically
- Secure money for retirement, with limited opportunities for leakage of retirement assets
- Portability of benefits, which will allow workers to retain benefits if they switch jobs
- Shared financing, with contributions from both employees and employers
- Lifetime benefits, so that retirement income cannot be outlived
- Spousal and disability benefits to provide protections against death or the inability to work
- Professional management of assets
- Low costs and fees

It is important to realize that there are already retirement plans in the United States that meet almost all of these criteria. In particular, the DB plans that provide retirement benefits to employees of state and local governments typically meet all of these criteria for a model retirement system. Also, multiemployer or Taft-Hartley plans in the private sector tend to fit this description.

The implication of this is twofold. First, public policy should strengthen the existing DB plans that already do a good job of offering retirement security to American families. Second, policymakers should adopt policies that will allow plans that do not yet meet these criteria to incorporate features that will bring them closer to this ideal.

The following discussion thus highlights these important plan features, shows how they work in multiemployer and public-sector DB plans, and draws policy lessons for the design of policy approaches to improving existing DB and DC plans.

Broad-based Coverage

Employees must simply meet the eligibility requirements of the DB plan to earn benefits in a DB plan. They are then automatically enrolled without having to make any active decisions. This truly "automatic" enrollment is a typical characteristic of all DB plans.

DC plans, on the other hand, often require employees to enroll themselves, and then make difficult decisions about how much to save and where to direct their investments.

Another DB feature that is reflected in proposals to restructure DC is universal coverage, which would make saving for retirement easier. However, there is generally a qualitative difference to DB plans. Universal coverage under DB plans automatically includes benefit accruals for vested employees, while proposals for universal DC coverage generally only include universal access to a savings account, i.e. the possibility of wealth creation without any assurance of contributions.

In passing the Pension Protection Act of 2006, Congress acknowledged this inherent flaw in DC plans and attempted to make automatic enrollment and efficient asset allocation easier. It is too soon to reach any conclusions about the law's effectiveness in increasing automatic enrollment in DC plans. Early indications show, however, that automatic enrollment is a feature of a growing share of existing DC plans. For instance, a survey by Hewitt Associates LLC (2008) showed that 44 percent of responding firms already offer automatic enrollment and 30 percent of those who do not are considering implementing it in 2008. Also, Deloitte (2008) reported that 42 percent of their survey respondents offered automatic enrollment in 2008, up from 23 percent just a year ago.

The evidence on the impact of automatic enrollment in the existing DC universe is too thin to evaluate how much faster employees, especially lower-income ones, are accruing retirement savings than in the past. Time will eventually tell how effective this policy move has been toward achieving greater retirement security for lower-income workers, for minorities, and for employees in small businesses.

Policymakers, though, should not be content with waiting for new evidence to emerge with respect to the impact of past policy changes. After all, the automatic enrollment features that were passed with the Pension Protection Act of 2006 only affect employers, who either already offer a qualified retirement savings plan or plan on offering one.

Instead, policymakers should consider added incentives for employers to offer access to qualified plans. The "automatic IRA" proposal does this by requiring that employers above a certain size offer access to direct deposits into an IRA, or by changing public saving incentives. In particular, two examples of proposals that move toward universal coverage in DC plans are "automatic IRAs" (Iwry and John, 2006), and "universal 401(k)s" (Sperling, 2005). Under the first plan, "automatic IRAs" would require that every employer with 10 or more employees would have to offer employees the opportunity of automatic payroll deductions into designated IRAs. To increase participation, Iwry and John (2006) suggest that this program could be coupled with automatic enrollment. To minimize costs, government administered accounts could be offered as the default investment (Iwry and John, 2006).

The second proposal goes a step further and pays attention to the particular vulnerability that low- and middle-class workers face because of low levels of savings. A universal 401(k), as proposed by my Center for American Progress Action Fund colleague Gene Sperling, adds progressive saving incentives, since all of these plans allow an employee to opt out of their coverage even if they were "automatically enrolled' (Sperling, 2005). Although this would again not automatically guarantee contributions, it would have the advantage of skewing savings incentives more toward low-income earners, where savings shortfalls are largest. The combination of universal access and progressive savings incentives could go a long way toward creating wealth for many middle-class families who currently do not save enough.

These proposals are directly targeted at increasing retirement savings coverage among employees who work for smaller businesses. As discussed before, the chance of being offered a plan when working for a smaller business is substantially lower than when working for a larger employer. Both the "automatic IRA" and the "universal 401(k)" proposals are intended to increase retirement savings coverage especially in this market segment. Coupled with automatic enrollment features, the hope is that increased coverage will also result in faster wealth accumulation.

Secure Money for Retirement

DB plans provide a secure source of income in retirement for a number of reasons. First, one's funds cannot be borrowed from and typically are not distributed as a lump-sum payment. That is, money under a DB plan will be there to provide a lifetime stream of retirement income.

Second, multiemployer DB plans and DB plans for state and local government employees reduce the impact that bankruptcy of an employer may have. In the case of multiemployer DB plans this is simply a function of many employers banding together to provide benefits. And, in the public sector, this is a result of the fact that state and local governments typically do not go bankrupt. This is sadly not always the case for single-employer, private-sector DB plans.

A third point is that pension plans tend to follow prudent investment principles and thus secure assets as much as possible. The security of assets in DC plans for future retirement income is, by comparison, compromised. Importantly, the vast majority of individuals in DC plans can borrow from their retirement accounts or withdraw funds before retirement age. Economists use the term "leakage" to describe assets that are drawn out of retirement savings plans for purposes other than providing retirement income (Weller and Wenger, 2008). According to one conservative estimate, a full 10 percent of all retirement wealth is lost due to leakage from DC plans (Englehart, 1999). Loans from DC plans have risen, especially to allow families to smooth over economic hard times, which will likely reduce their retirement income security (Weller and Wenger, 2008).

While employer default risk is generally not an issue for DC plans, individuals saving with those plans can be exposed to a number of well-known risks. These include longevity risk, idiosyncratic risk, and market risk among others. Moreover, these risks can be exacerbated by typical psychological responses of individual investors as the literature has demonstrated (Benartzi and Thaler, 2007). Policy can mitigate some of these risks by encouraging automated plan designs. I will return to this point further below.

This leaves the issue of potential leakages from DC plans due to loans. The policy response, however, should not be to eliminate loans from DC plans. It is important to recognize that employees typically take out a loan because they are financially strapped or because of an economic emergency, especially a sick family member (Weller and Wenger, 2008a). Consequently, the complete elimination of loans from DC plans may be simply impractical. If loans are prohibited, employees, who want to take out a loan because of an emergency, may request a hardship withdrawal instead.[6]

Policymakers, however, should encourage employers to limit the incidences for which employees can take out a loan, e.g. by mandating stricter limits on loans. Employers could discourage loans from DC savings plans by limiting the number of loans that can be taken out during a given time period—for example, only two loans in a five-year period. Employees could be required to wait for a minimum amount of time after a previous loan has been paid off before taking out a new loan. Employers could also further restrict the reasons for which a loan can be taken out and require that employees provide proof of those instances.

Portability of Benefits

Portability of benefits can be limited within some DB pension plans. It is important to realize, however, that this is a limited issue in the DB world. Single-employer DB plans may not offer lump sum withdrawal options, but more and more single-employer plans follow a cash balance plan design where a lump sum option is typically offered (Weller, 2005).

Further, public pension plans are responding to changing workforce needs in public service by offering much greater portability than in the past. Often, if employees move to another government position within the state, they are able to carry pension benefits with them. Should they move to other jurisdictions, they can usually purchase service credits (Brainard, 2008).

This portability also exists for most DC plans and in multiemployer plans. Little additional policy room exists, except that policymakers may want to consider reducing the maximum vesting period, as was done for cash balance plans in the Pension Protection Act of 2006. Shorter vesting periods will allow more mobile workers to accrue benefits where they may not accrue any right now, and thus enhance benefit portability.

Shared Financing

This is a typical characteristic of public-sector pension plans. The funding of state and local DB plans is a shared responsibility between employee and employer. Private- sector defined plans, by contrast, have employers typically finance the entire benefit. In 2004, for workers covered by Social Security, the median employer contribution rate was 7 percent of salary, while the employee contributed an additional 5 percent of salary (Munnell and Soto, 2007).

More could be done, however, to encourage employer contributions to DB plans. Two alternative approaches are available to accomplish this. First, policymakers could require a minimum employer contribution as is already the case or considered in some states for the employer contribution to existing DB plans (Weller et al., 2006). Second, funding rules for DB plans could allow for more smoothing of asset and liability values. This would reduce the pro-cyclicality of existing rules. Currently, the funding rules require larger contributions during bad economic times, when plan sponsors can often ill afford such additional requests on their cash flow. Inversely, current rules tend to lower the required contributions during good economic times, when employers can best afford contributing to their plans. An alternative set of funding rules would thus shift the funding burden from the bad to the good economic times without lowering benefit security. Weller et al. (2006) discuss two different valuation approaches to accomplish greater regularity of employer contributions. One of these approaches would allow for the smoothing of pension plan asset and liabilities over 20 years and require that employers contribute up to a specific level of assets above liabilities, e.g. 120 percent (Weller and Baker, 2005).

Further, the Pension Protection Act of 2006 has opened the door to more shared financing among DC plans. If employers offer the safe harbor option of automatic enrollment, they will have to also offer an employer matching contribution in addition to establishing automatically escalating employee contributions (Groom Law Group, 2006). More could be and should be done to encourage employer contributions, either as match or as non-matching contributions.

In addition, several proposals have included mandatory employer contributions in an effort to increase DC plan coverage. For instance, Weller (2007) develops a proposal called "Personal Universal Retirement" accounts. The costs and risks of these accounts would be kept low by managing the funds through a government entity, for example, the Federal Retirement Thrift Investment Board. Professional fund managers invest the funds of PURE accounts according to a worker's instructions. The investment options are the same as those for the Thrift Savings Plan to keep administrative costs to a minimum. Furthermore, universal employer contributions of at least 3 percent of earnings to a qualified pension plan or to a PURE account are required. These contributions would be pre-income tax, but subject to FICA. In addition, low-income workers would qualify for direct, non-elective contributions, while higher-income earners could qualify, up to a limit, for government matching contributions.

Also, Ghilarducci (2007) proposes "Guaranteed Retirement Accounts" which incorporate the low cost and effective risk management advantages of pooling assets, require coverage, and assure assets are paid-out in annuities. The GRAs are funded by a mandated 5 percent contribution on earnings up to the Social Security maximum, split evenly between the employer and employee. The contribution goes into a national fund comprised of individual accounts. Contributions are recorded in individual accounts and the account values represent an individual's claims on future benefits. Unlike conventional DC plans, the rates of return are guaranteed; the U.S. government will guarantee a rate of return of 3 percent with excess returns added, depending on the fund's earnings. Workers and retirees can add to the accounts at any time with pre- and post-tax dollars. By reconfiguring the current tax subsidies for retirement plans—that give people earning over $100,000 per year over $7,400 in tax subsidies while middle- and working-class workers receive practically nothing—each employee will receive a tax credit of $600. This tax rebate will go directly into workers' individual accounts and will add to national savings. The rebate will also soften the impact of a 5 percent mandated contribution for lower-income workers—most workers will pay much less than 5 percent. The efficient and well-managed Social Security Administration will administer the account. Qualified DB plans will be able to opt out of the mandate. At retirement, the accounts will be annuitized, and "opt to" withdraw a lump sum worth a maximum of 10 percent of the account value. The GRAs, combined with Social Security, are designed to guarantee the average worker 70 percent of pre- retirement earnings at retirement, approaching the level of 75 to 80 percent of pre-retirement income that is typically considered adequate by financial experts.

Lifetime Benefits

State and local DB plans are designed so that retirement income can never be outlived—retirees are guaranteed a paycheck for life. This is also the case with private-sector DB plans that have to offer an annuity benefit, even if it is as an alternative to a lump-sum distribution.

This is in stark contrast with DC plans. Here, the burden of managing one's retirement income, so that retirees do not run out of savings in retirement, falls mostly on the individual. In many cases, however, employees do not understand how much money they will need in retirement. The result is that many workers do not save sufficiently and face inadequate income in retirement. In order for a private-sector worker to purchase a modest annual annuity of $20,000, she must accumulate an estimated $260,000 in a 401(k). Yet, the median 401(k) balance for heads of households approaching retirement in 2004 was just $60,000 (Munnell and Soto, 2007). Further, Boston College researchers have found that, in part due to the shift from DB to DC plans in recent years, between 44 percent and 61 percent of households are at risk of being unable to maintain their living standards in retirement (Munnell et al., 2007).

A study by the National Institute on Retirement Security (Almeida and Fornia, 2008) recently quantified the additional cost that DC plans incur to provide the same retirement benefit to employees, who do not annuitize. Their calculations show that if employees self-annuitize, they will have to plan for the maximum life expectancy, instead of the average life expectancy. This increases the required contributions during the build-up phase of a retirement savings account by 15 percent. Consequently, policymakers could lower the implicit costs of DCs and thus deliver a better "bang for the buck" to beneficiaries if they could increase the share of savers, who annuitize their savings upon retirement.

Spousal and Disability Benefits

DB plans typically provide special protections for spouses of married beneficiaries, as well as disability benefits for active employees who are stricken by illness or injury that prematurely ends a career. Adding these types of benefits to DC plans, however, would require purchasing life insurance and disability insurance policies for beneficiaries. Addressing these ancillary benefits is beyond the scope of this testimony.

Professional Management of Assets

Public-sector plans and private-sector DB plans are managed by professionals with "considerable financial education, experience, discipline, and access to sophisticated investment tools" (Watson Wyatt, 2008). This is reflected, for instance, in the aggregate asset allocation data of public-sector DB pension plans. These plans tend to regularly rebalance their portfolio in response to price changes, show no signs of employer or trustee conflicts of interest, and appear to follow a best practices model by pursuing strategies similar to those employed by industry leaders (Weller and Wenger, 2008b).

The individualized nature of DC plans, however, means that these rely on self-management. As the Investment Company Institute found using 2006 year-end data, the bulk of 401(k) plan assets are invested in stocks (Investment Company Institute, 2007). When faced with the wide array of complicated and confusing choices that most DC plans have, workers may find themselves more vulnerable to the negative impacts of disturbances in the financial market. These can include a lack of diversification or an improper assessment of risk associated with their choices.

One response to this may be well-managed, balanced default investment options that allow participants in DC plans to take advantage of professional management of assets and thus help to avoid the commonly known pitfalls of individual investing (Benartzi and Thaler, 2007). The Investment Company Institute (2008) reported that lifecycle funds continued to experience growth from the end of 2007 through the first quarter of 2008, despite adverse overall market conditions. Most importantly, more widespread use of default investment options would encourage participants to diversify their assets and regularly rebalance them, thus avoiding the underperformance that often arises in DC plans due to an unintended "buy high, sell low" investment strategy. If the past is any indication, automatic investment options, such as lifecycle funds and model portfolios, will become increasingly prevalent. The Investment Company Institute (2007) reported that recent hires are more likely to choose these funds as their investment option.

Low Costs and Fees

Evidence shows that administrative costs are substantially higher for DC plans as compared to DB plans. An international study of plan costs finds that while, on average, fees can range between 0.8 percent and 1.5 percent of assets, larger institutional plans can reduce such fees to between 0.6 percent and 0.2 percent of assets (James et al., 2001). The UK Institute of Actuaries finds very high administrative costs for DC plans—of 2.5 percent of contributions and up to 1.5 percent of assets—leading to the equivalent of a 10 to 20 percent reduction in annual contributions. DB administrative costs, however, amount to just 5 to 7 percent of annual contributions (Blake, 2000). Similar differences exist in the United States, with DB plans incurring substantially lower fees than DC plans (Council of International Investors, 2006; Weller and Jenkins, 2007).

Almeida and Fornia (2008) estimate that the combination of professional management and lower fees reduces the costs of a DB plan relative to a DC plan by 21 percent annually. This is by far the largest area of economic inefficiencies in the existing DC structure.

Policymakers could help to substantially improve retirement income security by lowering fees and increasing the performance of DC plans, e.g. through more professional management and the avoidance of well-known pitfalls, such as lack of diversification, no regular contributions, and emotionally charged investment decisions ("buy high, sell low") among others.

A number of proposals have focused on the cost savings from pooling a large number of small accounts. Originally, Baker (1999) suggested that the government should establish a default investment option modeled on the Thrift Savings Plan for federal workers. Investment options would be limited to a small number of index funds. Because such a plan could take advantage of economies of scale and simplicity in investment options, management fees would be substantially lower than rates prevailing in private-sector plans (Congressional Budget Office, 2004).

This proposal is currently being studied at the state level as Washington state is studying the feasibility of the Economic Opportunity Institute's proposal for their Washington Voluntary Accounts proposal (Idemoto, 2002). This proposal has also been brought forth in other states, such as the Pennsylvania Voluntary Account proposal of the Keystone Research Center (Weller et al., 2006) or the Michigan Retirement Program Act of 2006 (Michigan Legislature, 2006).[7]

Conclusion

The decline in workers' retirement security is not a new occurrence, but rather a troubling trend, which is especially evident over the course of the current business cycle. We may have very well dodged a bullet last week with the actions taken by Congress and the administration. However, the long-term problems that were highlighted by the recent turmoil in the financial markets, including the overall weak retirement security of Americans overall, will not simply go away. The strength of America's workers' retirement security has been declining for many years and will likely continue to worsen, regardless of what happens as a result of last week's activities. It is because of this, and because of what America owes its workers, that we cannot stand idly by as this happens. We must instead improve retirement security by building a better DC plan and strengthening DB plans so that all Americans can look forward to a comfortable retirement and actually have the means to finance it. Importantly, there is no single "silver bullet" policy response. Instead, policymakers should take a pragmatic approach. They should consider all efficient policy options to increase the number of workers with a retirement savings plan, to raise retirement saving—especially among lower-income workers, those who work for smaller employers, and minorities—and to reduce the risk exposure of retirement savings.

References

Almeida, B. & Fornia, W. B. (2008). "*A Better Bang for the Buck: The Economic Efficiencies of Defined Benefit Plans*." Washington, DC: National Institute on Retirement Security.

American Enterprise Institute Public Opinion Studies. 2008. "*Economic Insecurity Update: Americans*' Concerns about their Jobs, Personal Finances, Retirement, Health Care, Housing, and More. "Washington, DC: AEI.

Austin Business Journal. (2008). "*Poll reveals Americans feel ill-prepared for retirement.*" June 23.

Baker, D. (1999). "*Pensions for the 21st Century." New York, NY: The Century Foundation.*

Benartzi, S. & Thaler, R. (2007). "Heuristics and Biases in Retirement Savings Behavior." *Journal of Economic Perspectives, 21(3)*, 81–104.

Blake, D. (2000). "Does it matter what type of pension scheme you have?" *The Economic Journal, 110(461)*, F46-F81.

Brady, P. & Sigrist, S. (2008). "Who Gets Retirement Plans and Why." Investment Company Institute Perspective 14, no. 2 (September).

Brainard, K. (2008). "*Redefining Traditional Plans: Variations and Developments in Public Employee Retirement Plan Design.*" Prepared for presentation at the Pension Research Council Symposium, May 1-2, 2008.

Board of Governors, Federal Reserve System. 2008. "*Release Z.1 Flow of Funds Accounts of the United States.*" Washington, DC: BOG.

Congressional Budget Office. (2004). "*Administrative Costs of Private Accounts in Social Security.*" Washington, D.C.: CBO.

Council of Institutional Investors. (2006). "*Protecting the Nest Egg: A Primer on Defined Benefit and Defined Contribution Retirement Plans.*" Washington, DC: CII.

Deloitte, (2008). "*401(k) Benchmarking Survey – 2008 edition.*" Zurich, Switzerland: Deloitte Touche Tohmatsu.

Employee Benefit Research Institute. (2008). "*EBRI Issue Brief #316: The 2008 Retirement Confidence Survey: Americans Much More Worried About Retirement, Health Costs a big Concern.*" Washington, DC: EBRI.

Englehart, G. V. (1999). "*Have 401(k)s Raised Household Saving? Evidence from the Health and Retirement Study.*" Paper 24. Aging Studies Program, Syracuse University.

Ghilarducci, Teresa. (2007). "*Guaranteed Retirement Accounts: Towards Retirement Income Security.*" Working paper, Department of Economics and Policy Studies, University of Notre Dame, Notre Dame, Indiana 46556. January

Government Accountability Office. (1997). "*401(k) Pension Plans: Loan Provisions Enhance Participation But May Affect Income Security for Some.*" Washington, D.C.: GAO.

Groom Law Group. (2006). "*Summary Comparison of Current Law and the Principal Provisions of the Pension Protection Act of 2006: Single-Employer Pension Funding Reforms and Cash Balance Provisions.*" Washington, D.C.: Groom.

Hewitt Associates, LLC. (2008). "*Survey Findings: Hot Topics in Retirement 2008.*" Lincolnshire, IL: Hewitt.

Idemoto, S. (2002). "*Washington Voluntary Accounts: A Proposal for Universal Pension Access.*" Seattle, WA: Economic Opportunity Institute.

Investment Company Institute. (2007). "*Research Perspective: 401(k) Plan Asset Allocation, Account Balances, and Loan Activity in 2006.*" Washington, DC: ICI.

Investment Company Institute. (2008). "*Research Fundamentals: The U.S. Retirement Market, First Quarter 2008.*" Washington, DC: ICI.

Iwry. M. & John, D. (2006). "*Pursuing Universal Retirement Security through Automatic IRAs.*" Working paper draft. Washington, D.C.: Retirement Security Project.

Jacobe, D. (2008a). "*A Shift in How Americans Plan to Fund Their Retirement.*" Washington, DC: Gallup.

Jacobe, D. (2008b). "*Fewer Americans Expect a Comfortable Retirement.*" Washington, DC: Gallup.

James, E., Smalhout, J. & Vittas, D. (2001), *Administrative Costs and the Organization of Individual Retirement Account Systems: A Comparative Perspective*, World Bank Policy Research Paper No. 2554, Washington, DC: World Bank.

Lake Research Partners and The Tarrance Group. (2008). "*George Washington University Battleground 2008 Poll.*" Washington, DC: Lake Research Partners.

Madland, D. (2008). "*Reforming Retirement: What the Public Thinks.*" Washington, DC: Georgetown University.

Michigan Legislature, (2006), Senate Bill 1329 (2006), Lansing, MI: Michigan Legislature.

Munnell, A. H. & Soto, M. (2007). "*State and Local Pensions are Different from Private Plans.*" Center for Retirement Research State and Local Pension Plans, No. 1. Boston College.

Munnell, A. H., Webb, A. & Golub-Sass, F. (2007). "*Is There Really A Retirement Savings Crisis? An NRRI Analysis.*" CRR Issue in Brief No. 7-11. Boston, MA: Boston College, Center for Retirement Research.

Purcell, P. (2008a). "*Pension Sponsorship and Participation: Summary of Recent Trends.*" Washington, DC: Congressional Research Service.

Purcell, P. (2008b). "Income and Poverty Among Older Americans in 2007." Washington, DC: Congressional Research Service.

Sperling, G. (2005). *The Pro-Growth Progressive*. New York, NY: Simon & Schuster.

Teixeira, R. (2008). "*What the Retirement Really Wants on Retirement and Social Security.*" Washington, DC: Center for American Progress.

Watson Wyatt. (2008). "Defined benefit vs. 401(k) plans: Investment returns for 2003-2006." *Watson Wyatt Insider,* 18(5).

Weller, C. (2005). "*Ensuring Retirement Income Security With Cash Balance Plans.*" Washington, D.C.: Center for American Progress.

Weller, C. (2007). "PURE: A Proposal for More Retirement Income Security." *Journal of Aging and Social Policy*. Winter.

Weller, C. & Baker, D. (2005). "Smoothing the Waves of Pension Funding: Could Changes in Funding Rules Help Avoid Cyclical Under-funding?", *Journal of Policy Reform 8*, No. 2:13 1- 151.

Weller, C. & Jenkins, S. (2007). "*Building 401(k) Wealth One Percent at a Time: Fees Chip Away at People's Retirement Nest Eggs.*" Washington, DC: Center for American Progress.

Weller, C., Price, M. & Margolis, D. (2006). "*Rewarding Hard Work: Give Pennsylvanians a Shot a Middle Class Retirement Benefits.*" Washington, D.C.: Center for American Progress and Harrisburg, PA: Keystone Research Center.

Weller, C. & Wenger, J. (2008a). "*Robbing Tomorrow to Pay for Today.*" Washington, DC: Center for American Progress.

Weller, C. & Wenger, J. (2008b), *Prudent Investors: The Asset Allocation of Public Pension Plans*, PERI Working Paper No. 175, Amherst, MA: Political Economy Research Institute.

End Notes

[1] It is also important to note that voters are not consistent, even when they profess support for a particular policy proposal (Madland, 2008). In other words, policymakers need to be mindful that promises of a single policy approach could quickly encounter opposition due to ideological predispositions. Instead, policymakers will need to take a pragmatic approach and promote all efficient policy options to increase retirement savings.

[2] The trends look very similar when the share of workers who have access to an employer-sponsored retirement plan is considered (Purcell, 2008a).

[3] Calculations based on Board of Governors (2008).

[4] Calculations based on BOG (2008).

[5] Calculations based on BOG (2008).

[6] In addition, the evidence suggests that the existence of a loan option may result in higher contribution rates (GAO, 1997). This link should weaken, if it hasn't already done so, if default employer contribution rates and automatic enrollment become more widespread, since an ever smaller share of employees will likely make a contribution decision that will differ from the employers' default option. This follows logically from the fact that automatic savings options are successful because they are taking advantage of people's inertia. Consequently, more people, who otherwise would not have contributed anything to their DC plan, will participate because it is the default option and will contribute the default contribution rate. The incentive provided by a loan option will thus be no longer necessary and policymakers limiting loan options will not inadvertently reduce savings incentives.

[7] This proposal was introduced as House Bill 6250 and Senate Bill 1329 in 2006, which both propose the Michigan Retirement Program Act. The act transfers Michigan's retirement plan to a private or non-profit entity no later than five years after this act is passed. Michigan's Department of Management and Budget would administer the retirement plan and would be the sole fiduciary of any plan. Administrative expenses would be paid by the participants and beneficiaries who have not closed their accounts.

In: Impact of Financial Crisis on Retirement Security
Editor: John J. Turner ISBN: 978-1-60692-960-5

Chapter 8

Saving Retirement in the Face of America's Credit Crises: Short Term and Long Term Solutions, Oral Testimony, Committee on Education and Labor, "The Impact of the Financial Crisis on Workers' Retirement Security," Rayburn House Office Building, Tuesday, October 7, 2008

Teresa Ghilarducci, Irene and Bernard L. Schwartz

As Congress reacts to the modern financial order changing forever, we should also realize that individual retirement plans based on that financial order, have also changed forever. In the last few weeks, we've been confronted with older worker and retirees' lives being turned upside down; their panic tops-off an already existing state of chronic anxiety about retirement futures. Much of both – the panic and anxiety - is caused by the corrosive effects of 401(k) and 401(k) – like plans[1], including IRA plans. 410(k) plans have not expanded pension coverage, increase the savings national rates; though they did add to the profits and growth of the financial sector and extracted ever increasing tax breaks from the Treasury.

Short Term Solution to the Retirement Crises

Short term, I propose that since 401(k) accounts and the like are financial institutions -- the bank about where 38% of the workforce[2] can intend to save for their retirement -- Congress let workers trade their 401(k) and 401(k) - type plan assets (perhaps valued at mid-August prices) for a Guaranteed Retirement Account composed of government bonds (earning a 3% return, adjusted for inflation). When the worker collects Social Security, the

Guaranteed Retirement Account will pay an inflation adjusted annuity, based on the accumulated funds.

How would this work? Take a 55 year old who had $50,000 in his 401(k) account in August and faces job loss and eroded assets because of the erosion of his retirement accounts.[3] Let him swap out the $50,000 for a guarantee of $500 per month[4]. The economy is probably in a recession, but a guaranteed income from his former 401(k) removes a source of financial anxiety, and -- this is not trivial – it end fruitless discussions with brokers and financial sales agents, who are also desperate for more fees and are often wrong about markets.

Long Term Solution to Eroding Retirement Income Security

Because there is a long run retirement crises, not in Social Security, but in the heavily tax-subsidized, private, voluntary, and commercial tier of our nation's retirement income security system, about half of workers will not have enough income after age 65 to replace, the bare necessity, 70% of their pre-retirement income according to Boston College's Retirement Risk Index. The erosion is primarily caused by Congressional bias towards 401(k) plans, their fundamentally flawed design and little regulation.

Going forward, I propose Congress establish universal Guaranteed Retirement Accounts and the federal government deposit $600 (inflation indexed) in those Guaranteed Retirement Accounts every year for every worker.

Every worker (not in an equivalent defined benefit plan) would save 5% of their pay into their Guaranteed Retirement Account to which the government pays a 3% inflation-indexed guaranteed return. Workers would earn pension credits based on these accumulations.

The 5% target comes from the basic math that an average earner saving 5% of pay over a life time with a guaranteed 3% rate of return plus inflation would supplement their Social Security benefits to achieve a 70% replacement rate at retirement. In other words had GRA been in effect instead of 401(k) plans an average earner reaching 65 today would have accumulated enough to pay about 1% for every year of service. (This rate is equivalent to the average defined benefit pension plan payout because it its inflation indexed.)

This basic math, though, comes up against the basic reality that many Americans can not afford to save that much. That is why workers' contributions would be mitigated by a $600 a year contribution from the federal government indexed for inflation which will be paid for by scaling back substantially the tax breaks for 401(k) type accounts. The $600 defrays the expense for most low and middle class workers (it pays for all the contribution for a minimum wage worker). Employers could top it off, pay a portion, and workers could add to it.

Advantages of a GRA?

First, this is a fiscally responsible plan. Rearranging tax breaks is revenue neutral, efficient and fair because the current tax breaks.[5] High-income earners get a much higher subsidy than anyone else because they are more likely to have a 401(k) and contribute more.[6]

This design has shocking results: 6% of taxpayers with incomes over $100,000 per year get 50% of the tax subsidies.[7] And, for all this effort, the nation gets no extra savings and workers no extra retirement security (see Appendix). At most, this complicated system creates economic activity when accountants happily transfer money between taxed accounts to tax-sheltered accounts and tax payers foot the bill.

Worse, the inefficiency is growing: the value of tax expenditures for DC plans is projected to grow 49 percent while those for traditional plans are projected to fall by 8.9 percent between 2009 and 2013. The sooner we admit that our 30 year experiment with 401(k) accounts has failed the sooner we can use these precious government subsidies efficiently and equitably.

Second, GRAs are responsible because they are prefunded. A government agency connected to the Thrift Savings Plan and Social Security (for administration efficiency) governed by trustees representing workers, business, and the public, invests the GRA contributions in a range of assets, like the sovereign wealth funds of Alaska, Alabama, New Mexico Wyoming, and many other nations do to ensure the federal government can pay a 3% inflation-indexed rate of return to the Guaranteed Retirement Account lifetime annuities.

Third, GRAs are universal;

Fourth, GRAs provide adequate retirement income and encourages people to save more;

Fifth, the money is locked away until retirement;

Sixth, the payout is for a person's life;

Seven, every America has the opportunity to save in a low cost, professionally managed account with guaranteed returns.

GRAs are better than automatic IRAs. Automatic IRAs add complicated requirements on small and medium sized employers. Automatic IRAs expand the risks workers already face in individual retirement account plans: the risks they won't save enough because of high fees and wrong in investments choices; the risk financial markets tank, the risk of inflation eroding income and that you will out-live your money. Automatic IRAs cause deadweight losses to the economy because, net of fees, 401(k) and other individual retirement accounts are among the lowest earning among all financial vehicles. Add the risks of preretirement - withdrawals, moral hazard, and adverse selection Automatic IRAs would entrench inefficiency and risk and a dollar of retirement income becomes more expensive to fund. Automatic IRAs are worse than nothing.

Disadvantages of GRAs

Scaling back 401(k) deductions going forward may put pressure on vendors to lower fees and boost returns. Also people like the option of saving at work for hardships. Fine, Congress may to subsidize precautionary savings but don't call them retirement accounts. Put them in a separate category.

Should we mandate savings in a recession? Yes, as long as fiscal policy provides for short term stimulus. No one is proposing we suspend Social Security taxes in recessions. Households need a source of disciplined savings over the business cycles; it is not the job of households to go in debt and spend wildly to get us the nation out of recessions. This ethos – debt-led consumer spending -- got us in the trouble we are in.

PREDICTED POPULARITY OF GUARANTEED RETIREMENT ACCOUNTS

Even before the financial crises of September 2008, workers are catching on that Congress needed to provide more secure sources of retirement income security.

Surveys show less than 50% of people think they will live comfortably in retirement and, crucially, that they bear personally responsibility for their supplements to Social Security benefits. Though they accept the responsibility -- they want the government to help.[8] Over 77% of people support mandated pensions.

In 2006, HSBC bank asked 21,000 workers in 20 nations what the government should do about the expense of aging societies- on average, workers preferred compulsory savings to any other policy. A third of Americans wanted the government to force them to save more for retirement; far fewer; 16% would support a tax increase; and, only 9% wanted the government to reduce benefits.[9]

In October 2007, a whopping 91% of Americans told a Wall Street Journal poll that the government should do something to secure retirement and 41% said they were not hearing enough from the Presidential candidates about retirement income issues.[10]

CONCLUSION

American workers know we have a short term and long term pension crises but it is not with Social Security but with the voluntary, self-directed, commercial- account - based pension system. The loss of retirement security is a reversal of fortune and the result of very specific flawed governmental policies that have been biased toward 401(k) plans, rather than the result of technological change or the logical consequences of global economic trends. That is the good news. Government policies eroded pensions government can help secure workers' retirement futures. If you implement the short term 401(k0 asset swap and Guaranteed Retirement Accounts, we can look back at the financial crises and bailout and know Congress did permanent good for workers' retirement income security.

Table 1

Tax Subsidies for Retirement Plans	2009 $ Billion	2009 growth to 2013 estimated
DB plans	$45.67 Billion	-8.9%
401(k) (325 B) Individual retirement plans and Plans covering partners and sole proprietors ("Keogh Plans")	$75. 70 Billion	49.5%

EBRI calculations Original data from Executive Office of the President, Office of Management and Budget, *Analytical Perspectives, Budget of the Untied States Government, Fiscal Year 2009* www.whitehouse.gov/omb/budget/fy2009/

APPENDIX

The Savings Paradox

Savings rates should be higher now than at any time in the history of the United States. The American workforce has never been more educated and people with more education save more. Middle-aged workers save more than any other age group and there are an estimated 73 million baby boomers in the U.S. who are between age 48 and 63 in 2008. High income people have higher savings rates the richest Americans have gained the most income since the 1990s. Further, as national income grows the demand for normal goods grow because when people have money they buy more of what they want Ipods, better health, and retirement "leisure:" witness the 1960s and 1970s, when, as the economy grew, older people lived longer AND retired earlier.[11] And, in an attempt to further increase retirement savings Congress has relentlessly expanded tax breaks forretirement savings since the 1980s.

The value of the favorable tax treatment for retirement savings is at an all-time high 110 B, while its effectiveness is at an all time low.

To be clear, saving is hard. Humans often lack the foresight, discipline, and investing skills required to sustain a savings plan. But human characteristics haven't changed as much as retirement savings as eroded.

The deep decline in national savings rates showed up in the 1990s when employers started to reduce their contributions into defined benefit pension plans[12], these plans were a main driver of national savings. The expansion of 401(k)-type plans did not boost savings for three reasons: they supplanted already existing defined benefit plans, were cheaper for the employer, and did not expand pension coverage to people who had no pension plan. This is surprising: although 401(k) - type plans are growing,[13] they don't expand pension coverage. Instead, they replace existing traditional pension plans. When groups of workers who ordinarily don't have pensions get them -- poultry workers, janitors, home-health care workers, etc. -- it is most likely because they are included in a newly negotiated collectively-bargained defined benefit plan.[14]

Defined benefit plans are institutionalized, contractual forms of saving that happen automatically at work. Workers have little discretion about whether to save or spend. Workers can't opt out, decide how much to invest, or take out lump-sum payments without difficulty. Even though 401(k) plans do not increase pension coverage nor secure retirement income, people like their portability and like to watch their individuals accounts grow. People do not like the financial and investment risks, or the risks of outliving their money, inherent in 401(k) accounts.

Therefore we understate the true spending on pensions because the U.S. Government maker uses "tax expenditures" – the value of the tax code's exemption of income generated for certain activities – to encourage workers and the nation's business owners to spend their income in socially approved ways.

In 2007, Social Security and Medicare cost $800 billion. Tax expenditures for retirement plans – traditional employer pensions (defined benefit plans), 401(k) plans, Individual Retirement Accounts, other savings vehicles dedicated for disbursement at older ages, and exemptions of Social Security and other federal pensions from tax – totaled over $156 billion in 2007.[15]

In 2004, taxes not collected on pension contributions and earnings equal a fourth of annual Social Security contributions and, at over $114 billion, are perversely larger than household saving of over $102 billion.[16] The tax breaks were supposed to expand pension coverage and increasing retirement security.

Pension tax breaks are deductions from income; high-income earners get more breaks than low-income workers. If a lawyer earning $200,000 makes a $1000 contribution to his 401(k) plan, he reduces his income tax by $350. If his receptionist, earning $20,000, makes the same $1000 contribution (which is much less likely), she will save only $150 in taxes. The Brookings Institution and Urban Institute calculate that the 3% of taxpayers with incomes over $200,000 per year get 20% of the tax subsidies.[17] And, for all this effort, the nation gets no extra savings. At most, this complicated system creates economic activity when accountants happily transfer money between taxed accounts to tax-sheltered accounts and tax payers foot the bill. The value of tax expenditures for 401(k) plans is projected to grow 49 percent while those for traditional plans are projected to fall by 2.1 percent between 2009 and 20013.[18] (The estimated tax expenditures for 401(k) plans, Individual Retirement Accounts, and Keogh plans in 2009 is estimated to be $75.1 billion and for defined benefit plans $45.7 billion.)

In sum, the shift towards 401(k) plans increases tax expenditures, does little to expand retirement savings, and favors workers who need the help least. All told, the tax subsidies are not meeting a public purpose. The top heavy benefits for 401(k) plans create a sad paradox: since 1999, tax expenditures for retirement plans grew by 20%, while retirement plan coverage fell.

401(k) plans Exist Because They are Cheaper for Employers; but they Earn Subpar Returns

If 401(k) plans are so bad why are there so many of them? Though workers don't gain much from 401(k) plans, some employers and Wall Street firms do. I followed 700 firms over 17 years and found that firms that adopted a 401(k) lowered pension expenses by 3.5 – 5% without sparking worker complaints.[19] Since 401(k) plans are voluntary, many (about 20%) workers who can don't bother to contribute "leave money on the table" by not accepting the employer match. Employers' contributions are 26% lower than they would be if everyone participated.[20] Employers could pay the match to every worker, as they do under defined benefit plans. Because workers have to trigger the match, and some don't, 401(k) plans boosts profits at the expense of retirement income security. Firms find sponsoring 401(k) plans is more profitable than sponsoring defined benefit plans. For firms, defined contribution plans are less costly, less risky, and can be funded with their own stock, not with hard cash.

Wall Street firms collect over $40.5 billion annually in 401(k) fees.[21] Yet, brokers and human resources often tell workers the fees on their accounts are zero. A good way to see what workers lose when they invest in a 401(k) plan rather than a group–based pension fund is to compare what each earns after fees are subtracted. A comprehensive study by Dutch and Canadian researchers Ron Bauer and Keith Ambachtsheer[22] found that U.S defined benefit plans – where individuals do not direct their own accounts – earned a 2.66% higher return NET of fees on equities than did retail mutual funds. In Canada, the skim was even higher;

the retail mutual funds earned 3.16% less. (These shortfalls are the averages for the 25 year period between 1980 and 2004.) The gap makes sense – investing in retail funds means investors pay for advertising, shareholder profits, and glossy brochures. Add the fact that workers buy high and sell low – because people follow the leaders and buy stock as its rising in value and sell when its falling -- and you have self-directed accounts earning much less. This isn't just a leakage, it's a levee break. Hidden from view, workers are unwittingly transferring huge sums of money to financial firms.

The unpublished report confirmed that the GRA 3% real rate of return was a conservative long-run estimate under a range of plausible investment strategies that a government agency could undertake and not take any substantial risk of underperforming.[23]

End Notes

[1] 401(k) – type plans are defined contribution plans include and include the following: 401(k) plans [about 80% of participants in defined contribution plans are in 401(k) plans]; profit sharing plans; money purchase plans; individual retirement accounts; and 403(b) plans which are 401(k) plans for employees in the public sector.

[2] Center for Retirement Research Boston College. 2004. "Eligibility and Participation in 401(k) Plans by Age, 2001 and 2004" http://crr.bc.edu/frequentlyrequesteddata/frequentlyrequesteddata.html accessed October 4, 2009.

[3] Note the macroeconomic destabilizing effects of 401(k) plans -- and all defined contribution plans – when asset values go down; people increase their job search just when jobs become scarce. This makes the recession worse.

[4] This is what the annuity would pay at a 3% inflation rate and a 3% real return.

[5] The GRA plan as written is budget neutral. If we allow tax breaks for the first $5000 in voluntary 401(k) contributions the plan will cost $25 billion. But know that accounts that allow hardship withdrawals are savings for hardship which is different from retirement income security.

[6] Because the tax subsidies come in the form of tax deductions and not credits they are regressive. For example, if a lawyer earning $200,000 makes a $1000 contribution to his 401(k) plan, he reduces his income tax by $350. If his receptionist, earning $20,000, makes the same $1000 contribution (which is much less likely), she will save only $150 in taxes.

[7] A good paper on the distributional effects of the tax expenditures for DC plans is Burman, Leonard E.,William G. Gale, Matthew Hall, and Peter R. Orszag. 2004a. Distributional Effects of Defined Contribution Plans and Individual Retirement Accounts. Washington, D.C.: Urban- Brookings Tax Policy Center.

[8] Madland, David. 2008. "Reforming Retirement: What the Public Thinks." For the Georgetown University conference on "The Future of Retirement Security." Held October 3, 2008. department of History

[9] HSBC Bank. "How should governments finance ageing populations" http://www.hsbc.com/1/PA11S5/content/assets/retirement/2006fornewsreleasefinal.pdf.) HSBC. 2007. "The Future of Retirement: What People Want." http://a248.e.akamai.net/7/248/3622/7d1c0ed7aa1 283/www. img.ghq.hsbc.com/public/groupsite/assets/retirement_future/2006_for_what_people_want.pdf (accessed online February 2, 2007).

[10] Bright, WSJ.com November 2007 online Harris personal finance poll

[11] Ghilarducci, Teresa. 2008. *When I am Sixty Four: The Plot Against Pensions and the Plan to Save Them.* Princeton University Press, Princeton, NJ. Chapter 1.

[12] Bosworth, Barry, and Lisa Bell. 2005. The Decline in Saving: What Can We Learn from Survey Data?" Unpublished draft written for the 7th Annual Joint Conference of the Retirement Research Consortium, "Creating a Secure Retirement" (Washington, DC, August 11-12, 2005). <http://www.bc.edu/ centers/ crr/dummy/seventh_annual.shtml>.

[13] 401(k) – type plans are defined contribution plans include and include the following: 401(k) plans [about 80% of participants in defined contribution plans are in 401(k) plans]; profit sharing plans; money purchase plans; individual retirement accounts; and 403(b) plans which are 401(k) plans for employees in the public sector.

[14] From 1999- 2005, the correlation between defined benefit coverage growth rates and pension coverage growth rates was 79%, while the correlation between defined contribution and pension coverage growth rates was a negative 10%. Ghilarducci. Teresa. 2006. "Future Retirement Income Security Needs Defined Benefit Pensions." Center for American Progress. www.americanprogress.org/kf/defined_benefit_layout.pdf

Back in 1981, Congress rejected President Carter's Pension Commission's call to reconsider the social value of these tax breaks and create a mandatory universal pension system (MUPS). Because they are designed to meet a social goal there were always conditions on these tax breaks. When the federal income tax was implemented in 1913, employer pension contributions were given special tax treatment only if the managerial plans included most of the rank and file. This is in direct acknowledgement that the tax breaks were targeted to the wealthy. The wrangling -- over how many tax breaks that higher income employees get in exchange for how many lower paid workers are in employer pension plans -- continues to this day and is part of a healthy process of assessing if the federal government tax breaks have the intended effects. Instead, in that same year, Congress satisfied the lobbyists for executives and made way for 401(k) plans by creating a section of the tax code which allowed workers to save, pre tax, in plans at work. After Wall Street firms and consultants successfully marketed 401(k) plans, the rest -- to use a shopworn phrase -- is a history we all know: 401(k)-type plans replaced traditional defined benefit (DBs) pensions.-- over 63% of pensions are DC plans; whereas, in 1975, most pensions were DBs.

[15] Employee Benefit Research Institute. 2008. "Facts From EBRI: Tax Expenditures and Employee Benefits: Estimates from the FY 2009 Budget." EBRI, 1100 13th St. NW #878, Washington, DC 20005. February

[16] See Bell, Elizabeth Adam Carasso and C. Eugene Steuerle, "Retirement Savings Incentives and Personal Savings,"*Tax Notes*, December 20, 2004.for this provocative insight.

[17] A good paper on the distributional effects of the tax expenditures for DC plans: Burman, Leonard E.,William G. Gale,Matthew Hall, and Peter R. Orszag. 2004. "Distributional Effects of Defined Contribution Plans and Individual Retirement Accounts."Washington, D.C.: Urban-Brookings Tax Policy Center.

[18] Employee Benefit Research Institute. 2008. "Facts From EBRI: Tax Expenditures and Employee Benefits: Estimates from the FY 2009 Budget." EBRI, 1100 13th St. NW #878, Washington, DC 20005. February

[19] Ghilarducci and Sun 2006. How **Defined** Contribution Plans and 401(k)s Affect Employer **Pension** Costs: 1981-1998." With Wei **Sun**. Journal of **Pension** Economics and Finance, 5(2): 175-196

[20] I used information from Munnell and Sundén. 2004. Munnell, Alicia, and Annika Sundén. 2004. *Coming Up Short: The Challenge of 401(k) Plans.* Washington, DC: Brookings Institution Press to get participation rates, average contribution levels by earnings, the distribution of employees by earnings (Calculated from the CPS (2003) to make the three billion dollar estimate. The average savings per worker is $156, calculated for their sample of over 800 employees in one firm that the employer saved over $250 per older worker who did not participate in the 40(k) even when they were eligible. Choi, James J., Laibson, David I. and Madrian, Brigitte C.,$100 Bills on the Sidewalk: Suboptimal Investment in 401(K) Plans(August 2005). NBER Working Paper No. W11554. Fidelity's (2004) annual report documents employers' match behavior.

[21] There are $2.7 trillion in 401(k) assets Employee Benefit Research Institute. 2007. "401(k) Plan Asset Allocation, Account Balances, and Loan Activity" An Information Sheet from the Employee Benefit Research Institute (EBRI). www.ebri.org/pdf/InfSheet.QDIA.23Oct07.Final.pdf. The average fee is over $700 per year and average fees are 1.5% of assets which equals $40.5 billion.

[22] Ambachtsheer, Keith, Bauer, Rob. 2007. "Losing Ground." *Canadian Investment Review*; Spring, Vol. 20 Issue 1, p8-14.

[23] My report for the Economic Policy Institute explains the GRA plan in depth Ghilarducci, Teresa 2007. "Guaranteed Retirement Accounts Toward Retirement Income Security" Economic Policy Institute, 1333 H Street, NW Suite 300, East Tower Washington, DC 20005-4707 (202) 775-8810, Economic Policy Briefing Paper #204, November 20.

In: Impact of Financial Crisis on Retirement Security
Editor: John J. Turner

ISBN: 978-1-60692-960-5

Chapter 9

THE EFFECTS OF RECENT TURMOIL IN FINANCIAL MARKETS ON RETIREMENT SECURITY BEFORE THE COMMITTEE ON EDUCATION AND LABOR, U.S. HOUSE OF REPRESENTATIVES

Peter R. Orszag

Chairman Miller, Ranking Member McKeon, thank you for inviting me to testify this afternoon about the effects of the crisis in financial markets on pensions and retirement security.

TURMOIL IN FINANCIAL MARKETS

Financial markets have experienced substantial stress for over a year. The turmoil emanated from the bursting of the housing bubble, which led to substantial losses on mortgage loans and mortgage-related securities. In part because the mortgage-related securities are complex and in part because future rates of defaults on the individual mortgages underlying those securities are hard to predict, financial markets have had difficulty gauging the magnitude of the losses on the securities. That opacity, in turn, has made it difficult to evaluate the financial condition of the institutions holding them.

Those problems have contributed to a broader collapse in confidence, leading to a general pullback from all types of risky lending. Financial institutions have become increasingly unwilling to lend to one another, creating stress in the interbank market for short-term loans that became particularly severe over the past several weeks. The issuance of corporate debt plummeted in the third quarter, and the commercial paper market has also been hit hard. Bank lending, which has thus far remained relatively strong, will likely be severely curtailed by the difficulties that banks are facing in raising capital. The general collapse in confidence is reflected in significant increases in risk spreads (or the difference between the interest rates charged on risky assets and those on Treasury securities). For example, the spread between the interest rate on corporate bonds with the lowest risk (AAA-rated bonds) and the interest rate on Treasury securities has risen by more than a percentage point since the middle of last year.

In sum, recent developments in financial markets represent a severe credit crunch, which could have devastating effects on the U.S. and world economies. In response, the Congress recently enacted a financial rescue package that, among other things, creates the Troubled Assets Relief Program (TARP), under which the Secretary of the Treasury is authorized to purchase, insure, hold, and sell a wide variety of financial instruments. The Congressional Budget Office (CBO) analyzed many aspects of that program in recent testimony before the House Budget Committee.[1]

The turmoil in financial markets has affected many aspects of the economy, including pensions. The most direct effect on pensions is through the prices of financial assets such as corporate equities and bonds. The Standard & Poor's 500 stock market index, for example, has fallen by more than 25 percent over the past year as the outlook for the economy and corporate profits has worsened.

Because the majority of pension assets are held in equities, drops in stock prices have had a significant adverse effect on pension plans.[2] Data from the Federal Reserve suggest that the decline in the value of financial assets cost pension funds (private-sector and public-sector combined) roughly $1 trillion—almost 10 percent of their assets— from the second quarter of 2007 to the second quarter of 2008 (the latest period for which data are available), and there has been a significant further drop in asset prices since then.

PRIVATE-SECTOR PENSION PLANS

The two principal types of pension plans are defined-benefit plans and defined-contribution plans. Over the past several decades, the private-sector pension system has shifted dramatically toward defined-contribution plans, such as 401(k) plans.

Defined-Benefit Pension Plans

In a defined-benefit pension plan, benefits are specified by a fixed formula unrelated to the value of the pension fund. The sponsor of the plan is generally responsible for financing the benefits and must therefore make larger contributions when the value of the assets held by the pension fund declines. By CBO's estimates, the value of the assets held by defined-benefit plans has declined by roughly 15 percent over the past year.

Because of the way the obligations of the plans are calculated, their funding position (that is, the relationship between their assets and liabilities) is also affected by the level of interest rates. Because payments will extend far in the future, the amount of funding today necessary to make those payments is adjusted for the time value of money by "discounting" them using certain interest rates. Those rates have increased over the past year, lowering the discounted value of plans' liabilities by roughly 5 percent to 10 percent and partially offsetting the drop in asset values.[3] Overall, according to CBO's estimates, defined-benefit plans' assets net of liabilities may have decreased by 5 percent to 10 percent over the past year.

Those developments have probably left private-sector defined-benefit pension plans' obligations exceeding their assets by a greater amount than last year. That circumstance could force employers to raise contributions to help trim the shortfall, reducing the cash that they have available for investment, hiring, or distribution to shareholders. However, such funding requirements are sensitive to future asset prices, which are highly uncertain given the turmoil in financial markets.

Defined-Contribution Pension Plans

Changes in asset prices have also affected the value of assets in defined-contribution pension plans. In those plans, the resources available to workers upon retirement depend directly on the value of assets in their plan account. Defined-contribution plans apparently are more heavily weighted toward stocks than defined-benefit plans are; over two-thirds of the assets in defined-contribution plans are invested in equities (either directly or through mutual funds). Because of that heavy emphasis on equities, the value of assets in defined-contribution plans may have declined by slightly more than that of assets in defined-benefit plans. To the extent households view balances in defined-contribution plans as part of their overall portfolio of wealth, a decline in those balances could lead people to reduce or delay purchases of goods and services. As described below, it could also lead some workers to delay their retirement.

State and Local Pension Plans

Public pension plans have also been affected by market developments. According to data from the Federal Reserve, for example, the assets held by state and local governments' pension plans declined by more than $300 billion between the second quarter of 2007 and the second quarter of 2008.[4] The composition of public-sector funds mimics that of corporate pension funds. Overall, about 60 percent of the assets in public pension funds are invested in equities, 30 percent in domestic fixed-income securities, 5 percent in real estate, and the remaining 5 percent in alternatives.[5]

Even before the current downturn, concerns had been raised about the funding levels of some public-sector pension plans. According to the most recent survey of public pension funds by the National Association of State Retirement Administrators, plans accounting for about 85 percent of the assets had funded ratios of 86 percent, on average.[6] (Funded ratios measure the degree to which assets and future contributions match current and future liabilities.) Some analysts have expressed concerns that reported funded ratios may be inflated because some public pension plans use relatively high discount rates when computing their future liabilities. The 20 largest public pension plans, which account for about half of all assets in such plans, have funded ratios of about 90 percent on average, but some smaller plans have funded ratios below 60 percent. Smaller plans, particularly those with lower funded ratios, may have a more difficult time weathering the decline in asset values.

Funded ratios have been steadily declining in recent years. In 2000, about 90 percent of public pension plans had funded ratios greater than 80 percent.[7] By 2006, that share had decreased to about 40 percent (though, again, a much larger share of large plans have funded ratios above 80 percent). Lower returns caused by a declining market and the economic slowdown, which will translate into lower corporate and personal income tax revenues, will exacerbate the downward trend in funded ratios.

Many public pension plans use actuarial methods that will mute the effects of recent changes in asset values on funded status. One of those methods is "smoothing," or valuing current assets on the basis of averages over recent years, rather than on current market values. That method generally causes the reported valuations to lag behind the market; in the current environment, it can cause reported valuations to be higher than current market values.

Although the laws governing state and local pension plans vary, significant drops in funded ratios could trigger requirements for higher contributions to the plans from state and local coffers or from public-sector employees at a time when tax collections are also waning.

HOUSEHOLDS' ASSETS AND RETIREMENT BEHAVIOR

Asset prices affect households not only through pension plans but also through their other holdings. Although most households have few assets outside retirement plans, those assets are still substantial in the aggregate. In 2006, income from assets outside retirement plans provided almost as much income for households with elderly members as pensions did: Pensions provided 18 percent of the aggregate income for the population age 65 and older, and asset income accounted for 15 percent.[8] Social Security provided 37 percent, on average; and earnings, 28 percent.

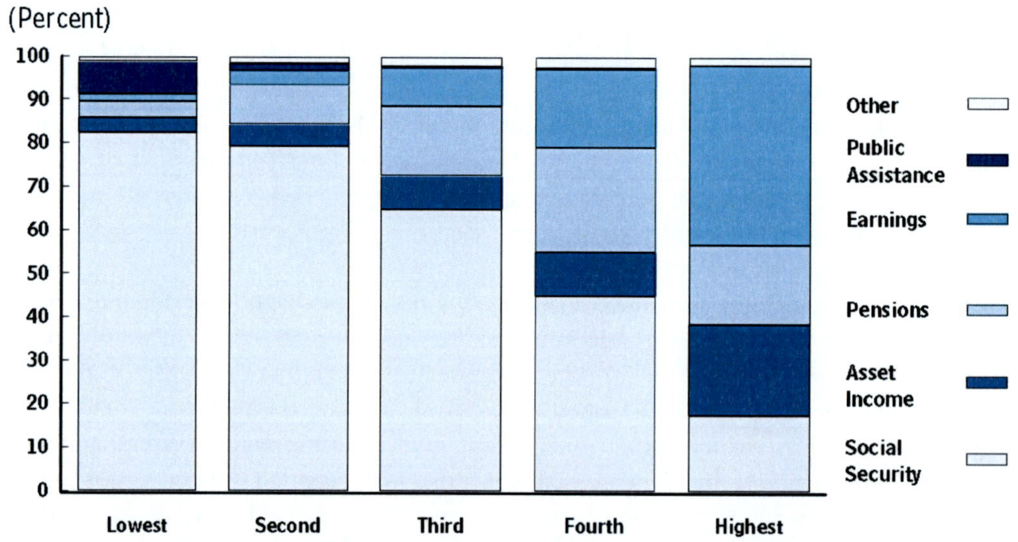

Source: Congressional Budget Office based on data from the Federal Interagency Forum on Aging-Related Statistics, *Older Americans 2008: Key Indicators of Well-Being*.

Figure 1. Sources of Income for People Age 65 and Older, by Income Quintile, 2006

The shares of income coming from pensions and asset income vary widely across the income distribution, however (see Figure 1). Among households with elderly members, those in the lowest income quintile obtained only 4 percent of their aggregate income from pensions and just 3 percent from asset income. At the other end of the distribution, households in the highest quintile received 18 percent of their income from pensions and 21 percent from asset income.

Some people on the verge of retirement might respond to a decline in financial markets by working longer. In 2006, 36 percent of people age 65 and older were in families with earnings; that share could rise somewhat over the next few years, both because of underlying trends in the labor market and because of the recent turmoil in financial markets.

Older workers' participation in the labor force decreased during the 1970s and early 1980s but has increased since then (see Figure 2). The labor force participation rate of workers 55 to 64 years old, for example, fell from about 62 percent in 1970 to 54 percent in 1986 and then rose steadily, to nearly 64 percent in 2007.[9] The rate for workers age 65 and older followed a similar pattern and is at nearly the same level today as it was in 1970. Moreover, the fraction of people age 55 and older who work full time grew from about 22 percent in 1990 to nearly 30 percent in 2007 (see Figure 3).

Studies that have examined the impact of the stock market boom of the 1990s and the subsequent decline of the early 2000s on retirement decisions show mixed results. One paper, for example, found no evidence of an increase in the retirement age among people in households owning stocks after the stock market decline of 2000.[10] Another paper, however, showed that survey respondents who held corporate equity immediately prior to the bull market of the 1 990s retired, on average, 7 months earlier than other respondents.[11]

MITIGATING FINANCIAL MARKET RISKS

Although severe stresses in financial markets almost inevitably cause wrenching adjustments by workers and employers, the risks can be attenuated by sensibly designing pension plans. For example, although workers enrolled in defined-contribution plans may not be able to avoid bearing the risks associated with broad price changes in financial markets, they can avoid unnecessary risks associated with a lack of diversification. Such unnecessary risks can arise, for example, by overweighting portfolios with individual stocks rather than diversified index funds.

In recent years, many firms have adopted automatic enrollment in defined- contribution pension plans.[12] Such automatic enrollment dramatically increases participation rates, especially for subgroups such as workers with low income, for whom participation is otherwise very low. Perhaps of more relevance to a discussion of financial market risks, however, the Pension Protection Act of 2006 requires that the allocation of assets by automatic-enrollment pension plans meet certain criteria that protect against excessive risk for participants. As a result, pension assets for automatically enrolled workers tend to be weighted toward more-diversified portfolios. Such protections against nondiversified investment portfolios can help avoid excessive exposure to financial market risks. By design, however, workers in defined- contribution plans must inevitably bear the risks associated with broad market fluctuations.

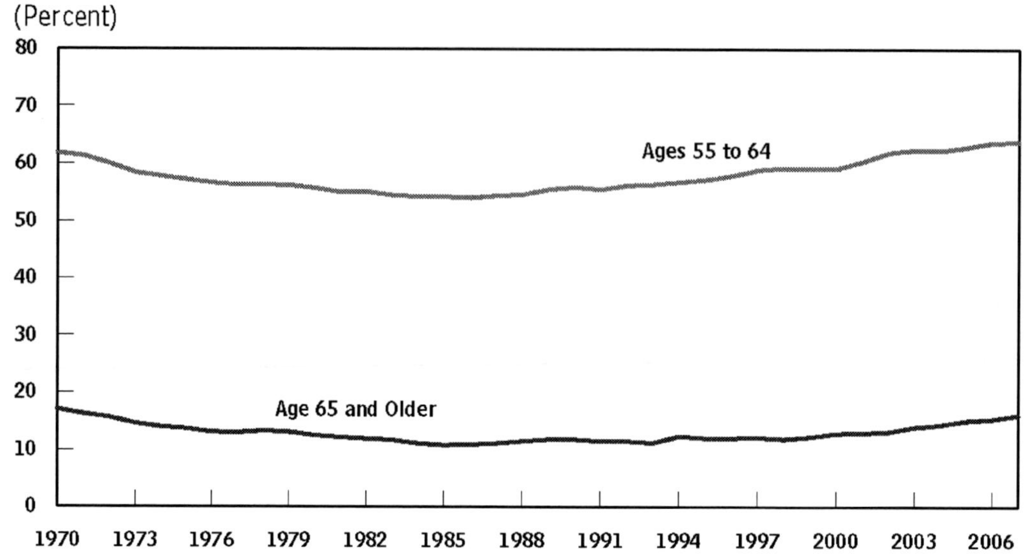

Source: Congressional Budget Office based on data from the Bureau of Labor Statistics.

Figure 2. Percentage of Older People Participating in the Labor Force, 1970 to 2007

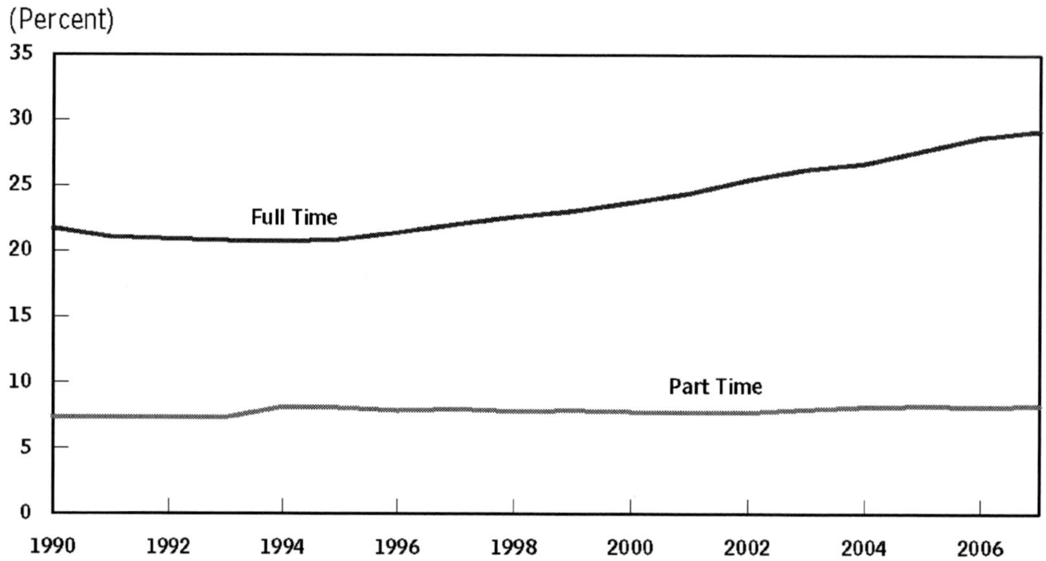

Source: Congressional Budget Office based on data from the Bureau of Labor Statistics.

Figure 3. Percentage of People Age 55 and Older Working Full- or Part-Time, 1990 to 2007

End Notes

[1] Statement of Peter R. Orszag, Director, Congressional Budget Office, before the House Committee on the Budget, *Federal Responses to Market Turmoil* (September 24, 2008).

[2] One important question is whether the current value of stocks represents a temporary dip or a permanent adjustment to a new, lower value. Economists have not resolved empirically the question of whether stocks

depart only temporarily from some relatively stable average. However, some evidence suggests that stock prices tend to revert to a more stable long-run value after particularly sharp declines. See, for example, James M. Poterba and Lawrence Summers, "Mean Reversion in Stock Prices," *Journal of Financial Economics*, vol. 22, no. 1 (1988), pp. 27–59; Eugene Fama and Kenneth French, "Permanent and Temporary Components of Stock Prices," *Journal of Political Economy*, vol. 96, no. 2 (1988), pp. 246–273; and Jeremy J. Siegel, *Stocks for the Long Run* (New York: McGraw Hill, 2007).

[3] That calculation is based on the yields on corporate debt rated A or higher, which have increased over the year, according to several indexes.

[4] Federal Reserve, Flow of Funds Accounts of the United States, Table L. 119, "State and Local Government Employee Retirement Funds," September 18, 2008, available at www.federalreserve.gov/ releases/Z1 /Current/z1r-4.pdf.

[5] Alternatives include private equity, hedge funds, currency, commodities, and cash.

[6] See Public Fund Survey, "Actuarial Funding Levels," (2007), available at www.publicfundsurvey. org/publicfundsurvey/index.htm.

[7] Statement of Barbara D. Bovbjerg, Director, Education, Workforce, and Income Security, Government Accountability Office, before the Joint Economic Committee, published as Government Accountability Office, *State and Local Government Pension Plans: Current Structure and Funded Status*, GAO-08-983T (July 10, 2008).

[8] Federal Interagency Forum on Aging-Related Statistics, *Older Americans 2008: Key Indicators of Well-Being*, available at agingstats.gov/agingstatsdotnet/Main_Site/Data/Data_2008.aspx.

[9] Based on data from the Current Population Survey compiled by the Department of Commerce's Bureau of Labor Statistics, available at www.bls.gov/data/#employment.

[10] Courtney C. Coile and Phillip B. Levine, "Bulls, Bears, and Retirement Behavior," *Industrial and Labor Relations Review*, vol. 59, no. 3 (April 2006), pp. 408–429, available at digitalcommons. ilr.cornell.edu /cgi/ viewcontent.cgi?article=1218&context=ilrreview.

[11] Julia Lynn Coronado and Maria G. Perozek, "Wealth Effects and the Consumption of Leisure: Retirement Decisions During the Stock Market Boom of the 1990s," FEDS Working Paper No. 2003-20 (Federal Reserve Board, May 2003), available at ssrn.com/abstract=419721.

[12] See, for example, William E. Nesmith, Stephen P. Utkus, and Jean A. Young, "Measuring the Effec- tiveness of Automatic Enrollment," Vanguard Center for Retirement Research, vol. 31 (2007).

In: Impact of Financial Crisis on Retirement Security
Editor: John J. Turner
ISBN: 978-1-60692-960-5

Chapter 10

Testimony for the House Education and Labor Committee, "The Impact of the Financial Crisis on Workers Retirement Security," October 7, 2008

Jack VanDerhei

Mr. Chairman and members of the committee, thank you for your invitation to testify today on the impact of the financial crisis on retirement security. I am Jack VanDerhei, research director of the Employee Benefit Research Institute. EBRI is a nonpartisan research institute that has been focusing on retirement and health benefits for the past 30 years. EBRI does not take policy positions and does not lobby.

Although there is no clear definition of the time period for the "current financial crisis," this testimony defines it as the first nine months of 2008. During that time, major equity indexes were negative, with the S&P 500 Index losing 19.29 percent. Fixed-income investments fared much better during this period, with the Lehman Aggregate Index gaining 0.63 percent and three-month T-bills gaining 1.54 percent.

The impact of the current financial crisis on defined benefit (pension) plans is impossible to quantify, but it is obvious that a marked reduction in funding ratios and/or increase in volatility may make continued sponsorship of these plans less attractive under some forms of pension accounting modifications. Moreover, the Pension Protection Act of 2006 (PPA) has established specific restrictions with respect to freezing of accruals, plan amendments and lump- sum distributions as a function of funding ratios. Recent estimates from Watson Wyatt projected that pension plans would be 84 percent funded as of Sept. 24, down from 91 percent in the second quarter. [1]

Considerably more is known about the immediate impact of the current financial crisis on defined contribution plan (primarily 401(k)) participants. It should be emphasized that while older employees have average equity allocations that are lower than their younger counterparts (and hence are thought by some to be less vulnerable to negative returns in the equity markets), their average account balances are significantly larger and therefore have more to lose in a significant downturn.

Research has shown that a worker's age is a major factor in his or her ability to recover from an economic downturn. Holden and VanDerhei (2002) simulated the likely impact of a major bear market—defined as three consecutive years of a –9.3 percent annual return—on the overall (nominal) replacement rates that could be provided by "401(k) accumulations" as a function of when the downturn occurred during the employee's tenure with the plan sponsor.

Based on a median replacement rate of about 51 percent of final income, the modeled three-year downturn would result in a lower replacement rate for 401(k) participants in the lowest-income quartile of only –3.2 percentage points at the beginning of their career, or –7.5 percentage points for those in mid-career (ages 39–41), or –13.4 percent for those at the end of their career.[2]

However, building and/or modifying a simulation model that is able to quantify the likely impact of a market downturn on eventual retirement income is a lengthy process. Consequently, attention is typically focused on how a decline in the financial markets has impacted the average defined contribution plan balances. For purposes of this testimony, EBRI has taken the most recent information in the EBRI/ICI 401(k) database (year-end 2006) and used employee-specific information as well as financial market indexes[3] to estimate the percentage change in average account balances among the 2.2 million 401(k) participants present from year-end 1999 through year-end 2006, by age and tenure for three different periods:

- January 1, 2008, through October 1, 2008 (Figure A);
- January 1, 2007, through October 1, 2008 (Figure B); and
- January 1, 2000, through October 1, 2008 (Figure C).

This "consistent sample" of 401(k) participants was created several years ago in the annual analysis of EBRI/ICI 401(k) data to provide an estimate of changes in average annual account balances that was not biased downward by job turnover of 401(k) participants.

For this analysis, contributions in 2007 and the first nine months of 2008 were assumed to be equal to the participant's 2006 contributions, adjusted for changes in average national wage during that period. Loan and withdrawal behavior were estimated based on 2006 experience for similar employees. These estimates will be biased if asset allocation of current contributions, or contribution, loan or withdrawal behavior has changed since 2006 (presumably in response to the fluctuations in the financial markets).

However, Hewitt Associates, LLC, has recently stated that participants "appear to be taking a long-term investment strategy for their 401(k) retirement assets by choosing an asset allocation and staying with it," and that net transfer activity was "consistently low."[4] Fidelity has also reported that participants did not increase their borrowings from 401(k) accounts in 2007 and the first half of 2008.[5] However, hardship withdrawals are on the rise in the first half of 2008 compared with the first half of 2007.[6]

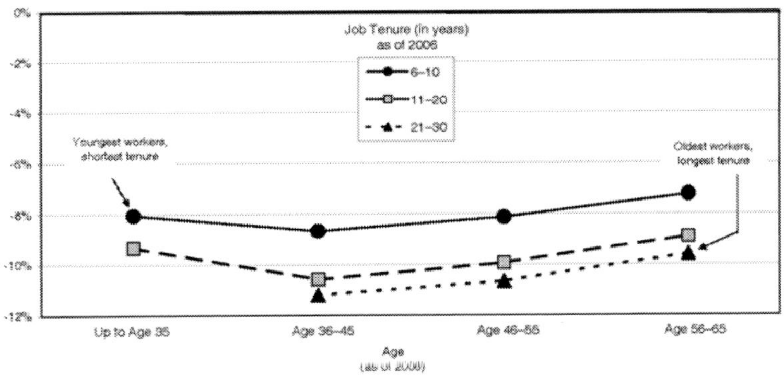

Sources: 1999 and 2006 Account Balances: Tabulations from EBRI/ICI Participant-Directed Retirement Plan Data Collection Project.
2007 and 2008 Account Balances: EBRI estimates. The analysis is based on a consistent sample of 2.2 million participants with account balances at the end of each year from 1999 through 2006.
[a] Age and tenure groups are based on participant age and tenure at year-end 2006.

Figure A. Change in Average Account Balances Among a Consistent Sample of 401(k) Participants, by Age and Ten ure,[a] Jan. 1, 2008–Oct. 1, 2008

Figure A shows that for *the first nine months of 2008,* the percentage loss in average account balances among 401(k) participants in the consistent sample varies from a low of –7.2 percent for the oldest cohort (age 56–65 in 2006) with the shortest tenure with the 401(k) sponsor (six to 10 years in 2006), to a high of –11.2 percent for the youngest cohort with 21–30 years of tenure. The reason that this particular group has the lowest average loss is a function of the reduced equity exposure they take (on average), as well as the larger ratio of contributions to account balance given their relatively short tenure. The group with the largest average loss is those young enough to still have a relatively large equity exposure in their accounts, compared with the others in the long-tenure cohort.

Figure B shows the *cumulative experience for 2007 as well as the first nine months of 2008*. In 2007, the S&P 500 index return was positive (5.5 percent) but not nearly enough to offset the losses in the first nine months of 2008. In this case though, the cohort with the most favorable cumulative percentage change were the youngest workers with the shortest tenure (7.2 percent increase). Even though they were still more aggressively invested (on average) in a down market, the ratio of contributions to account balances was sufficiently larger than the older cohorts in the short-tenure category. Once again, the worst performers were the youngest cohort with 21–30 years of tenure (a decline of –2.2 percent).

Figure C broadens the time span under analysis and shows that, even with the financial market setback suffered so far in 2008, the percentage change in average account balances from January 1, 2000, through October 1, 2008, was significantly positive for all groups and all age cohorts in the two shortest-tenure categories to have at least doubled their account balances (in nominal terms). The largest increase was again experienced by the group with the youngest workers and shortest tenure (706 percent), in large part due to greater weight of their contributions as compared with investment earnings or losses. Those having the lowest increase were the oldest workers with the longest tenure (55 percent); however this number needs to be interpreted carefully in light of the ability of many employees to start taking in-service distributions from their plans at age 59-½.

Additional Research Needed to Better Understand How the Financial Crisis Is Affecting 401(k) Participants

The primary reason for using the consistent sample as the basis for analysis in the preceding section is the current inability to track workers as they move from one 401(k) sponsor to another, and/or to follow their retirement assets if the 401(k) assets are rolled into an IRA. EBRI is currently in the process of enhancing our research capabilities to allow this kind of data to be captured. This will allow linking of accounts across data providers within our universe of individual account plans, resulting in a more complete and accurate retirement picture—such as measuring the effect of rollovers, multiple accounts, job turnover, account leakage, etc.

Another research topic that is urgently needed to better understand the vulnerability of 401(k) participants to volatility in the equity markets deals with the topic of target date funds. Figure D shows for the consistent sample described above the asset allocation distribution of 401(k) participant account balances to "equity" by age, as of December 31, 2006. Equity in this figure is defined as the percentage of the participant's 401(k) funds in equity funds, company stock and the equity portion of balanced and/or target date funds. The figure shows that 43 percent of young 401(k) participants (those 35 or younger in 2006) have 90 percent or more of their 401(k) assets in equities (broadly defined). Another 15 percent of this cohort have 80–90 percent of their assets allocated in this fashion, and another 11 percent have 70–80 percent allocated to equities.

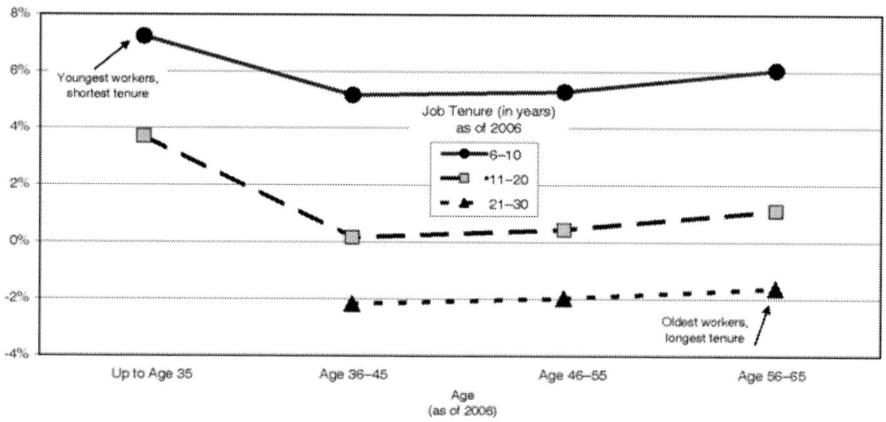

Sources: 1999 and 2006 Account Balances: Tabulations from EBRI/ICI Participant-Directed Retirement Plan Data Collection Project.

2007 and 2008 Account Balances: EBRI estimates. The analysis is based on a consistent sample of 2.2 million participants with account balances at the end of each year from 1999 through 2006.

[a] Age and tenure groups are based on participant age and tenure at year-end 2006.

Figure B. Change in Average Account Balances Among a Consistent Sample of 401(k) Participants, by Age and Tenure,[a] Jan. 1, 2007–Oct. 1, 2008

Although many asset allocation models and/or financial advisors may suggest that extreme concentrations to equities for the young cohorts would be acceptable, it is less certain that those approaching retirement would receive similar recommendations. Nevertheless, Figure D shows that more than 1 in 4 (27 percent) of the oldest 401(k) participants (age 56-65 in 2006) had 90 percent or more of their 40 1(k) assets in equities. Another 11 percent had 80-90 percent in equities, and 10 percent had 70–80 percent in equities.

Target date funds with automatic rebalancing and a "glide path" ensuring "age-appropriate" asset allocation are likely to become much more common after full implementation of PPA, with the expected increase in automatic enrollment for 401(k) plans and the attendant interest in QDIAs. Based on unpublished EBRI research, the average equity allocation for target date funds designed for individuals in the 56–65 age range was 51.2 percent at year-end 2006. That would imply that approximately one-half of the consistent sample participants in the age 56–65 age category would have had at least a 20 percent reduction in equities at year-end 2006 if they were allocated 100 percent to target date funds.[7]

EBRI is currently conducting an analysis of target-date funds for defined contribution plans. This project will incorporate three distinct, but interrelated, phases. The first phase will provide an empirical analysis of the use of target-date funds in 401(k) plans. The second phase will focus on a conceptual analysis of the optimal construction of target-date accumulation principles for defined contribution plan participants, including the extension of these principles into the decumulation phase. The third phase will include an empirical analysis of the choice of target-date funds by plan sponsors and correlates with employee demographics and plan design variables. Hopefully, the additional insights generated by this research will assist in providing a more informed asset allocation for those nearing retirement age.

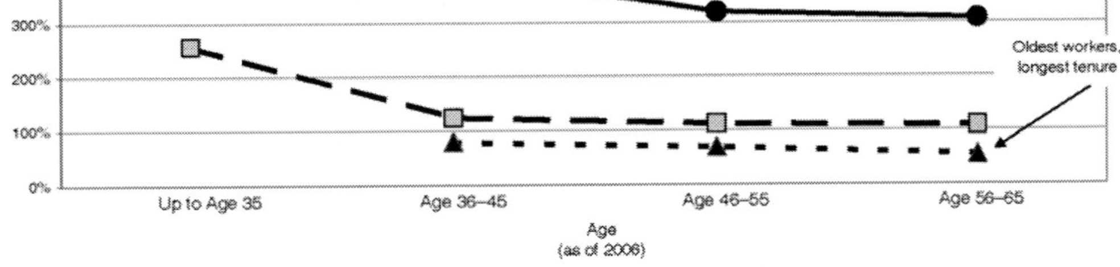

Sources: 1999 and 2006 Account Balances: Tabulations from EBRI/ICI Participant-Directed Retirement Plan Data Collection Project.

2007 and 2008 Account Balances: EBRI estimates. The analysis is based on a consistent sample of 2.2 million participants with account balances at the end of each year from 1999 through 2006.

[a] Age and tenure groups are based on participant age and tenure at year-end 2006.

Figure C. Change in Average Account Balances Among a Consistent Sample of 401(k) Participants, by Age and Tenure,[a] Jan. 1, 2000–Oct. 1, 2008

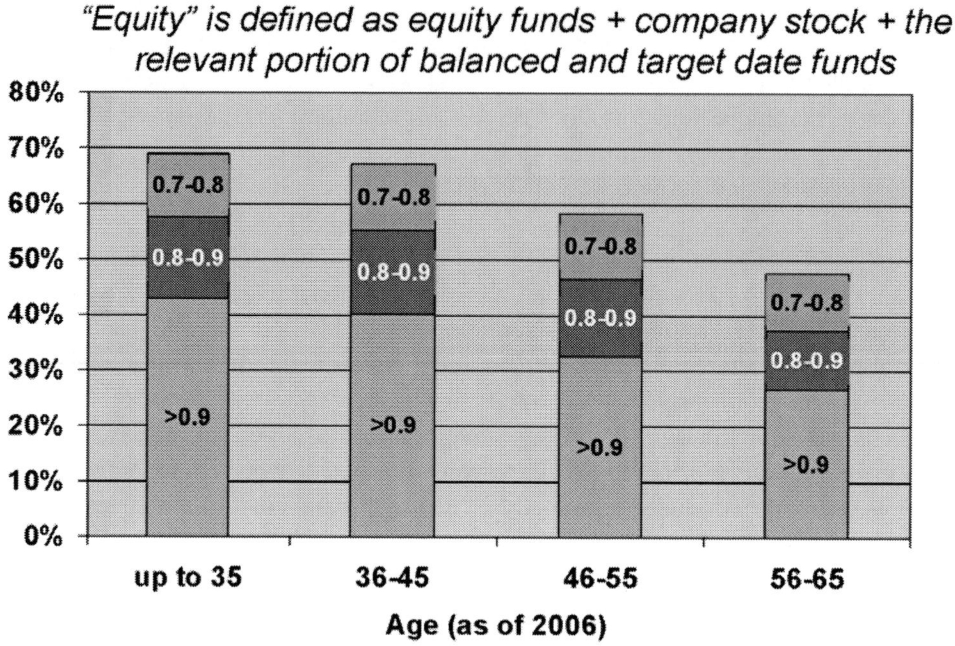

Source: Tabulations from EBRI/ICI Participant-Directed Retirement Plan Data Collection Project. The analysis is based on a consistent sample of 2.2 million participants with account balances at the end of each year from 1999 through 2006.

Figure D. Dec. 31, 2006 Asset Allocation Distribution of 401(k) Participant Account Balances to "Equity," by Age

End Notes

[1] "DB plan funding and DC allocations steady," Pensions and Investments, Sept. 29, 2008.

[2] For 401(k) participants in the highest income quartile, the median replacement rate decreased by 3.7 percentage points if the market downturn would occur at the beginning of the career. The decrease was estimated to be 10.4 percentage points if it took place at the middle of the career. If the market downturn took place at the end of the career, the estimated decrease was 17.7 percent. These percentage point decreases for this group were based on a median replacement rate of 67.2 percent of final income, assuming a regular stochastic simulation of equity returns.

[3] For purposes of this analysis, investment returns were proxied by one of the following three index returns: S&P 500 Index, Lehman Aggregate Index or three-month T-bills. These asset classes were assumed to have fees of 45, 45 and 75 basis points, respectively.

[4] "DB plan funding and DC allocations steady," *Pensions and Investments,* Sept. 29, 2008.

[5] *Financial Week,* "Workers swearing off 401(k) loans, says survey," (Aug. 19, 2008). Online at www.financial week.com/apps/pbcs.dll/article?AID=/20080819/REG/860878

[6] *Business Insurance,* "Large Plan Providers Report Drop in 401(k) Loans by Workers – But Hardship Withdrawals on the Rise As Employees Struggle with Economic Difficulties Arising Out of Credit Crisis," (Sept. 8, 2008). Online at www.businessinsurance.com/cgi-bin/article.pl?articleId=25814&a=a&bt=large+plan+providers

[7] It is possible that some of these participants were invested in company stock via employer matching contributions that were not able to be diversified.

In: Impact of Financial Crisis on Retirement Security
Editor: John J. Turner
ISBN: 978-1-60692-960-5

Chapter 11

STATEMENT BY ROBERTA TIM QUAN, U.S. HOUSE COMMITTEE ON EDUCATION AND LABOR, GEORGE MILLER "THE IMPACT OF THE FINANCIAL CRISIS ON WORKERS' RETIREMENT SECURITY," OCTOBER 22, 2008

Roberta Tim Quan

My name is Roberta Tim Quan from San Pablo, California. I am 74 years old. I retired as an elementary school educator from the Richmond School system in the East Bay. It was a rewarding career having instructed over 700 children in a span of 25 years.

In the era of the 1960's, my husband John, was employed at the Lawrence Berkeley Laboratory. With our combined income, we were able to save almost an entire salary. Classically, expenses were for home mortgages, auto loans, utilities, health care, food and clothing, and a university education for our son. The cost of living was most reasonable at this time. Thus, planning for our future retirement, each month funds were payroll deducted into a 403(b) plan.

Throughout the years, we looked forward to a reasonable retirement with the accumulating nest egg. Typically, retirement activities would include travel plans, lunch with friends, time spent with our granddaughter, and perhaps a health club membership. At age 70½, I began taking the Required Minimum Distribution from my 403(b) plan in the sum of about $550 per month. All appeared well.

Those best laid plans did not occur due to several life - altering factors in the last several years

1. In 2000, John was diagnosed with Alzheimer's. I was his care giver for six years. As he entered the severe stage, I could no longer handle the 24/7 regimen. John was placed in a residential care home two years ago. The expenses ran $6,000/mo that breaks down to $200/day. Recently I transferred him to a facility costing $3,800/mo down to $127/day. One of his Alzheimer's medications runs $1,100 for a 3 month's

supply. A recent bout with pneumonia resulted in a week's hospitalization for John. An unexpected and unbudgeted expense.

2. Within the last few years, expenses have sky-rocketed. A litany of cost increases; i.e., health, home and auto premiums, fuel costs, utility bills, food bills, property taxes, etc. The cost of living was out of sight but the income remains modest. Overwhelmingly, the only alternative was to pare down expenses to the bare-bone where ever possible.
3. The recent unstable financial crisis is having a devastating effect on my life. As of the current July-September report, my 403(b) account has sustained a loss of $38,000. I do not look forward to the next quarterly report. My situation is in shambles with expenses exceeding income. A life-time of savings in catastrophic decline is demoralizing.

The bottom line is that I am retired and unable to re - earn the lost funds. I am now faced with the insecurity of outliving my rapidly diminishing 403(b) account. And that is worrisome for John and my future. The word "fear" looms on the horizon.

I thank you for the opportunity to voice my concerns. It is my hope that concrete action will be initiated to rectify this economic crisis as soon as possible. We have reached critical mass.

In: Impact of Financial Crisis on Retirement Security
Editor: John J. Turner
ISBN: 978-1-60692-960-5

Chapter 12

STATEMENT BY JERRY BRAMLETT, BENEFITSTREET, INC., COMMENTS PRESENTED TO THE HOUSE EDUCATION AND LABOR COMMITTEE, U.S. HOUSE OF REPRESENTATIVES "THE IMPACT OF THE FINANCIAL CRISIS ON WORKERS' RETIREMENT SECURITY," OCTOBER 7, 2008

Jerry Bramlett

Chairman Miller and Congressman Andrews, thank you for this opportunity to speak before you today on this critical issue facing tens of millions of Americans. My name is Jerry Bramlett, President and CEO of BenefitStreet. BenefitStreet is the nation's premier, independent recordkeeping and plan administration firm with more than 1,500 clients across the country. We are a pioneer in the creation and delivery of innovative 401 (k) solutions and leading- edge technology.

Throughout my 25 years of building the largest independent 401 (k) plan recordkeeping firms in the country, I have experienced every aspect of the retirement industry up close and have developed a good deal of insight as to how we got to this point and where we should go from here.

401(k) plans have become the retirement foundation for most Americans. In terms of promoting savings they have been immensely successful. Low to moderate income individuals are twenty times more likely to save when they are offered a 401 (k) plan at work. However, the current financial crisis has certainly highlighted the fact that 401 (k) participants—whose 401(k) account represent their sole retirement savings—bear all the investment risk. This contrasts to defined benefit plans, where the burden of funding, asset allocation and investment selection belong to an employer under the constraints of fiduciary laws. With 401 (k) plans, all the risk associated with asset allocation and investment selection is shifted to the ill-prepared worker.

401(k) participants are understandably concerned about their retirement savings. The recent substantial decline in the market impacts almost every one of them. The pain is particularly acute for those participants closer to retirement whose retirement income expectations have been significantly impaired possibly resulting in the need to postpone retirement.

Given that most 401(k) participants are not investment experts, there is a danger that many of them will over react to this market downturn—I want to caution against this. For participants with still many years to retirement, a drastic abandonment of equity positions in their retirement account will only serve to lock-in as of yet unrealized losses. Markets do go up and down and 401(k) participants must try to remember to think long-term. It is important to remember, that as recently as September 1987 the market declined over 25 percent—3,000 points in today's terms. In the following years the market rebounded and reached even higher levels. In fact, according to the economist Jeremy Seigel there has never been a 20-year period where the stock market has yielded negative returns.

Let me emphasize, exchanging the equity investments in your retirement account for Treasury bills is not a sound long-term investment strategy and will subject retirees to substantial inflation risk. This also applies to participants who are nearing or entering retirement who will likely be managing retirement assets for some time – on the average another 15 years or so. Even these closeto-retirement employees can impair their long-term retirement assets by acting precipitously.

To be clear, I am certainly not saying that those with 401(k) accounts should do nothing. Current participants should take the time to evaluate where their new contributions are being invested and perhaps consider less volatile investments that will allow them to better diversify their entire account. By changing where these new contributions are being invested 401(k) participants should seek to have an appropriately diversified allocation of assets with a good balance of both equity and fixed income investments.

Which brings me to another point, I do not believe the 401(k) system is doing an adequate job of educating participants as to how they need to invest their account as they get closer to retirement. The practical impact of a substantial market decline on a 64-year old worker months away from retirement can be very different than the impact on a 50-year old 15 years from retirement. If the retirement account of the 64-year old is heavily invested in equities, the impact of a major market decline on retirement income expectations can be devastating. However, if that same account had been properly diversified with a greater emphasis on fixed income securities, the impact of a major market decline may very well be manageable. Although the advent of target-date investment funds based on a participant's age has greatly helped in this regard we need to do more. I would recommend that Congress instruct the Department of Labor to develop educational materials specifically for 401(k) participants that have reached age 50 to assist them in better managing their account in preparation for retirement.

The current financial crisis has also revealed some fundamental flaws in the 401(k) system that I want to highlight.

- Given how this turmoil is impacting large insurance companies and banks, plan fiduciaries need to make sure that, when offering a so called stable value or fixed interest fund, such funds are diversified across a large number of financial institutions. What we have learned over the last couple of weeks is that very large institutions can fail no matter how stable they may appear on the surface. In other words, just like plan participants need to diversify the investments in their account, plan fiduciaries need to diversify the investment providers used by the plan. As far as I know, the Department of Labor places no emphasis on this.

- You may not be aware that since this recent financial crisis began certain retirement funds—such as real estate investment funds—have announced that they are frozen and not available for distributions to participants due to the illiquid nature of the underlying assets. This means that current participants cannot change their investment and retirees cannot get distributions. Congress should examine whether investments subject to this susceptibility are appropriate.
- You also may not be aware that if a financial institution holding retirement plan assets becomes troubled, a plan fiduciary may practically or even contractually not be able to do anything about it. For example, there are retirement assets invested in insurance contracts that can be subject to significant back-end loads or may even have contractual prohibitions on taking the money out. I have seen contracts with such prohibitions lasting as long as five years. Congress should consider whether such restrictions should be permissible with respect to retirement plan assets.
- You should also be concerned about funds that may be advertized as "low-risk" (such as short term bond funds) but, in reality, contain high- risk assets that cause the fund to perform more like an equity fund in a down market. It is important not only to know how a fund is labeled, but what is actually in a given fund regardless of what it may be called.
- Finally, it is critically important that we not forget the issue of fee transparency. While the market is going down, hidden fees are still being assessed. As this Committee has already heard, hidden 401(k) fees can have an enormous impact on a participant's retirement account. Those opposed to fee transparency argue that only the overall net return on an investment should matter. So what is their argument when the return is a substantial loss compounded with hidden fees? Mr. Chairman, I fully support the bill (H.R. 3185) that you introduced this year enhancing 401(k) fee transparency and very much hope you will continue your quest to shine the light on hidden fees in the new Congress.

Thank you for this opportunity to testify on these important issues. I will be happy to answer any questions you may have.

In: Impact of Financial Crisis on Retirement Security
Editor: John J. Turner
ISBN: 978-1-60692-960-5

Chapter 13

CHAIRMAN MILLER STATEMENT AT COMMITTEE HEARING ON "THE IMPACT OF THE FINANCIAL CRISIS ON WORKERS' RETIREMENT SECURITY," OCTOBER 22, 2008

Education and Labor Committee

WASHINGTON, D.C. – *Below are the prepared remarks of U.S. Rep. George Miller (DCA), chairman of the House Education and Labor Committee, for a field hearing on "The Impact of the Financial Crisis on Workers' Retirement Security."*

Good morning.

Today this Committee is holding our second hearing to examine how the current financial crisis is affecting retirement savings – one of the many issues creating enormous anxiety for Americans in our ailing economy.

We started this investigation last week, as part of a series of hearings the House is conducting to investigate the causes of the financial crisis, and what additional steps are needed to protect homeowners, workers, and families.

What we heard confirmed that while this crisis may have started on Wall Street, it's Main Street that stands to suffer the most.

Peter Orszag, the director of the Congressional Budget Office, told us that American workers have lost more than $2 trillion in retirement savings over the last fifteen months – an astonishing loss that could lead workers to delay their retirement. Yesterday, the Center on Retirement Research found that $4 trillion in retirement savings has been lost. Over the last year, $2 trillion in 401(k)s and IRAs and $2 trillion in defined benefit plans has been lost.

Several experts also told us that workers closest to retirement could suffer the most from this financial tsunami.

A survey released last week by the AARP found that one in five middle-aged workers stopped contributing to their retirement plans in the last year because they had trouble making ends meet. One in three workers has considered delaying retirement.

A new poll by the Washington Post/ABC News also captured this growing strain on older workers.

More than 60 percent of respondents ages 50 to 64 were not confident that they'd be able to save enough money to carry them through retirement – a steep drop in confidence that cuts across Americans from all income brackets.

Overall, less than half of all respondents said they will be able to save enough for a secure retirement.

But while the housing and financial crises are intensifying retirement insecurity, we also know that workers' retirement savings have been declining for quite some time.

Rising unemployment, stagnating wages and benefits, and a shift away from more traditional defined-benefit pension plans have been making it much harder for workers to save for retirement while juggling other expenses.

Now, the number of investors taking loans on their 401(k) accounts is increasing. And hardship withdrawals are also increasing.

T. Rowe Price estimates a 14 percent increase in hardship withdrawals just in the first eight months of 2008.

And, all the signs point to an increased frequency of 401(k) loans and hardship withdrawals in the coming year.

Even more troubling, just this week, our Committee obtained preliminary estimates showing that the Pension Benefits Guaranty Corporation – the government agency that insures private sector pension plans – lost at least $3 billion in equities in the last fiscal year.

This dramatic loss represents a swing of more than $6 billion from the previous year. It's likely that the agency's losses will be substantially worse once numbers from September are reported.

These estimates raise serious questions about a controversial new investment policy that the agency recently approved that shifts assets from fixed-income securities into more risky securities like real estate.

At this time of severe economic uncertainty, it's crucial that this agency be a responsible steward of these funds which pay pensions to workers whose plans have been terminated. The PBGC needs to be accountable to the millions of Americans who count on the agency to protect their retirement.

More than ever before, there is an urgent need to help Americans strengthen their retirement savings.

Taxpayers subsidize 401(k) plans by $80 billion dollars annually. For a taxpayer investment of this size, we must ensure that the structure of 401 (k)s adequately protects the nest eggs of participating workers.

At a minimum, we know that much greater transparency and disclosures in 401(k) investment policies are needed, to protect workers from "hidden" fees that could be eating deeply into their retirement accounts.

And with seniors poised to suffer the most from the current economic turmoil, we must suspend an unfair tax penalty for seniors who don't take a minimum withdrawal from their depleted retirement accounts, like 401 (k)s.

Last week, Rep. Andrews and I called on Secretary Paulson to immediately suspend this unfair penalty.

We'll also push to enact legislation based on a bill Rep. Andrews recently introduced, so that seniors who have seen their retirement savings evaporate don't get penalized for trying to build those savings back up.

Today our Committee will hear additional ideas about what we can do to strengthen and protect Americans' 401(k)s, pensions, and other retirement plans. We will also hear from Roberta Quan and Steve Carroll – two retirees who are grappling with significant losses to their retirement savings. I'd like to thank them for sharing their personal stories and all of our witnesses for joining us.

As other committees' hearings have revealed, many of the Wall Street titans responsible for this crisis have still escaped with their plush perks, lavish spa trips and golden parachutes intact. This is an outrage.

For too long, the Bush administration anything goes economic policy allowed Wall Street to go unchecked.

As we look at how we can rebuild workers' retirement savings and our nation's economy, the Democratic Congress will continue to conduct this much-needed oversight on behalf of the American people.

Being able to save for retirement after a lifetime of hard work has always been a core tenet of the American Dream. We can't allow the promise of a secure retirement for workers to become a casualty of the financial crisis.

Thank you.

In: Impact of Financial Crisis on Retirement Security
Editor: John J. Turner
ISBN: 978-1-60692-960-5

Chapter 14

CHAIRMAN MILLER STATEMENT AT COMMITTEE HEARING ON "THE IMPACT OF THE FINANCIAL CRISIS ON WORKERS' RETIREMENT SECURITY," OCTOBER 7, 2008

Education and Labor Committee

WASHINGTON, D.C. – *Below are the prepared remarks of U.S. Rep. George Miller (D-CA), chairman of the House Education and Labor Committee, for a committee hearing on "The Impact of the Financial Crisis on Workers' Retirement Security."*

Good afternoon.

Last week, Congress approved an emergency rescue plan in response to the worst financial crisis our country has seen since the Great Depression. We know that this plan alone will not magically turn the economy around. But we are confident that without it we will not have the chance to move forward.

We insisted that the plan include strong protections for taxpayers and tough accountability – neither of which was included in the President's original request to Congress.

Immediately after the plan was approved, Speaker Pelosi announced that the House would conduct a series of hearings to investigate the causes of the current financial crisis and what steps we should take next to protect homeowners, workers and families struggling today.

As part of that commitment, the Committee on Education and Labor today is holding a hearing to explore how this financial crisis is impacting the retirement security of American families.

Yesterday, the House Oversight and Government Reform Committee launched the first of many oversight hearings examining the toxic mix of corporate greed, recklessness, and deregulation that created this financial crisis.

During his testimony, Lehman's CEO, Mr. Fuld, showed no remorse for his catastrophic mismanagement of the company. In fact, he repeatedly denied responsibility for running the storied Lehman Brothers investment house into financial oblivion.

He refused to admit that his own reckless management – and his industry's success of keeping regulators at bay – directly contributed to this historic financial crisis that is costing taxpayers, shareholders, and the nation's current and future retirees billions of dollars from their nest eggs.

All the while, he insisted on taking obscene multi-million dollar bonuses for his executive teammates.

Unlike Wall Street executives, American families don't have a golden parachute to fall back on.

It's clear that their retirement security may be one of the greatest casualties of this financial crisis.

The current financial and housing crises are stripping wealth from American families at a record rate.

A new poll just found that 63 percent of Americans are worried that they will not have enough savings for their retirement. Tragically, they may very well be right. Due to the collapse of the housing market and the financial crisis, trillions of dollars that Americans were counting on has been lost.

Americans were counting on much of this wealth for their retirement. Now it is gone – as is their ability to adequately fund their retirement.

Even before the current meltdown, middle-income families were losing ground due to the decline in middle-class wages over the last decade – making it harder for them to save for their retirement and family emergencies.

Retirement and financial experts now predict that retirees and older workers who rely on financial investments for retirement income may suffer more than any portion of the American population in the coming years.

According a survey released today by the AARP, one in five middle-aged workers stopped contributing to their retirement plans in the last year because they had trouble making ends meet. One in three workers has considered delaying retirement.

Now, the number of investors taking loans on their 401(k) accounts is increasing. And hardship withdrawals are also increasing.

T. Rowe Price estimates a 14 percent increase in hardship withdrawals just in the first eight months of 2008.

And, all the signs point to an increased frequency of 401(k) loans and hardship withdrawals in the coming year.

It makes sense that more Americans will be raiding their retirement accounts as they deal with rising unemployment and increasing costs of basic necessities.

Unfortunately, these drastic measures taken by workers today will have a long-lasting impact by significantly reducing account balances once these workers reach retirement age.

Over the past 12 months, more than a half trillion dollars have evaporated from 401(k) plans as a direct result of the crisis in the markets.

Some experts say that it will take as long as 3 years to recover market losses in 40 1(k)-style accounts – but only if the market turns around soon.

Just like consumer directed retirement plans, traditional pension plans are not immune from the financial crisis.

Although pension plans hire professional money managers and are required to be diversified, these plans will likely lose value as a result of the weak performance of the investment markets.

Sophisticated pension funds lost 20 to 30 percent of their value during the 2001 recession and took several years to overcome those losses.

We must keep our eye on these plans and I await further data on the health of our nation's pensions.

While this crisis began on Wall Street, much of the financial burden will ultimately be borne by Main Street. And this did not happen overnight.

With the Republicans' help and armed with their powerful lobbyists, Wall Street cunningly held off fair regulations by Congress, arguing that Americans would be better off if left to their own devices.

As Congress continues our investigations into this crisis, we cannot allow those responsible to emerge unscathed. The American people are paying the price of this go-go, Wild West approach to governing.

One cost will be the concern that our nation's workers will not have sufficient savings to ensure a secure retirement after a lifetime of hard work. In the coming months, this committee will examine what measures may be needed to ensure a safe and secure retirement for workers, retirees and their families.

For starters, we know that 401(k) holders lack critical information about how their money is managed and what fees they pay.

I'm here to say right now, those days are over.

We must have more transparency in 401(k) investment practices. The Wall Street veil of secrecy must end.

I would like to thank all of our witnesses for joining us today. I look forward to their testimony.

And I expect that we will be back here repeatedly until we can ensure greater security for the retirement of hard-working Americans.

In: Impact of Financial Crisis on Retirement Security
Editor: John J. Turner
ISBN: 978-1-60692-960-5

Chapter 15

Written Testimony of Matthew D. Hutcheson, Independent Pension Fiduciary on "Are Hidden Fees Undermining Employee Retirement Income Security?" Presented to the Committee on Education and Labor, U.S. House of Representatives, March 6, 2007

Matthew D. Hutcheson

Introduction

Very few matters of social importance are more complex than the one before you today. This particular issue is not only about uncovering obscure dollars unscrupulously extracted from the account balances of America's workforce, but it is also about correcting the culture that has permitted the problem to thrive in the first place. This written testimony will explain what the culture is, why it exists, how it has evolved over time, how it violates basic economic principles, the integrity of rules of fiduciary prudence, the exclusive benefit rule under ERISA, and other common sense practices that are critical for delivery of expected results from employer defined contribution retirement plans.

The American Worker Is Hurt by What He Can't See

"If we make a few rough calculations, the importance of the topic will be very clear. The SEC estimates in Concept Release 33-8349, that 1% of the average fund's investment return disappears each year due to brokerage expense, execution costs, and transaction spreads.

Other industry sources indicate that an additional .50% slips away via "revenue sharing payments." The impact on the average American is profound.

"Consider two thirty year old workers who each invest $3, 000 annually into their 401(k) programs. American #1 's 401(k) program is run according to stringent fiduciary principles and earns 7.5% annually. However, American #2's 401(k) is operated by conflicted, sales driven entities and only earns 6% annually after the aforementioned return erosion. The table below details the results.

> *"Even though both employees contributed the same amount and took the same investment risk, American #2 must work an additional seven years to make up for the lack of fiduciary oversight in his 401(k) plan."*[1]

The difference in hidden fees costs American worker #2 nearly **$500,000** during the illustrated period of time. This issue is about real people, real money, and the quality of their lives later in life. Consider the impact on American worker #2's ability to pay for health care, prescription drugs, home repairs or even groceries. If actuarial tables hold true, today's retiree may need to be prepared to live a quarter century longer than his grandparents did.

BACKGROUND

A "401(k)" is a Qualified Retirement Plan

Qualified retirement plan assets pursuant to Internal Revenue Code ("IRC") section 401(a) are held in trust pursuant to IRC §501(a) and the Employee Retirement Income Security Act ("ERISA") §403(a) *exclusively* for the future benefits of participants and beneficiaries. 401(k) plans enable employees to take wages and bonuses in cash, or *defer* them into the trust, and hence are often referred to as "employee deferrals." All sources of contributions, whether from the employer or employee, plus investment earnings of "401(k)" plan investments are subject to the same rules of trust administration, governance, and fiduciary prudence that apply to all employee benefit plans defined by ERISA §3(3), including traditional profit sharing, and traditional pension plans.

ERISA – Employee *Retirement Income Security*

The purpose of a retirement plan, including 401(k) plans, is to provide *future income* for retired American workers. Those who are charged with the management of a qualified retirement plan must do so with an eye single to this purpose and none other. Such an individual is a "fiduciary."

Rules of Fiduciary Prudence

As it relates to the issue at hand, the following fiduciary axioms have consistently held true:

Year	American # 1 – Fiduciary 401(k)Earning 7.5%	American # 2 - Hidden Fee 401(k)Earning 6%
10	$45,624	$41,915
20	$139,658	$116,978
30	$333,463	$251,405
40	$732,902	$492,143
47	$1,244,260	$766,694

- Fiduciary based decisions secure future retirement income.
- Non-fiduciary based decisions diminish future retirement income.
- Hidden and excessive fees exist in part because both types of decisions (fiduciary based and non-fiduciary based) exist simultaneously within 401(k) and other similar plans, complicating and obscuring a fiduciary's ability to understand his duties and to properly discharge them.

This written testimony will focus solely on 401(k) and similar plan assets held in trust, pursuant to IRC §501(a) and ERISA §403(a). Therefore, rules of Fiduciary Prudence are a fundamental component of this discussion because trusts are governed and managed by fiduciaries. True prudent fiduciary practices should deliver optimal results. Poor or partial fiduciary practices will deliver sub-optimal or even poor results.

Fiduciary principles and ideals are not obscure, nor are they difficult to learn and understand. In fact, modern rules of fiduciary prudence have existed for nearly two hundred years. However, in the United States, the primary way fiduciary responsibilities are taught to sponsors of retirement plans is through the financial industry. Since an important element of fiduciary governance is monitoring those who provide services to a retirement plan, strangely enough, we have accepted a system where those being monitored are teaching those who are doing the monitoring, and doing so according to their philosophies and standards, with a particular objective in mind.

The current 401(k) culture essentially couples the "fox teaching the rooster how to guard the hen house" with a perceived governmental "get out of jail free card" (i.e. DOL regulation 404(c)). The effect of adopting these two "cultural" elements has, over time, caused 401(k) plans to be governed through the blending of fiduciary and non-fiduciary practices and philosophies.

Therefore, resolving the issue of hidden, obscure, and excessive fees is wholly dependent on bifurcating fiduciary elements and practices from the non-fiduciary ones within the 401(k) industry. Then, logic will reveal that any fees paid for non-fiduciary services and practices are unnecessary, and hence excessive. Furthermore, these are the fees that are hidden because they simply cannot be justified when viewed through the lens of true fiduciary prudence. In short, if fiduciaries eliminate non-fiduciary practices in their 401(k) plans, they will immediately eliminate hidden and excessive fees. To argue otherwise would suggest that

401(k) plans are only "partially" subject to fiduciary prudence, and hence are only a "partially" qualified plan.

Conceptually, it is as simple as that – but in practice, it is far more difficult.

Complexity

The hidden fee problem in 401(k) and similar plans is actually a mysterious Gordian knot consisting of trust law, tax law, public policy, doctrines of fiduciary prudence, financial principle, economic principle, and perhaps the lack of discipline to defer control and gratification until actual retirement. It is difficult to see the ends of the rope, and very few know how to unravel it. In addition, many who might discern how to unravel it have strong incentives not to do so.

It is widely accepted that 401(k) and similar arrangements are the way most Americans will invest for retirement. Therefore, it is incumbent upon us all to be absolutely certain there are no unnecessary obstacles (whether intentional or unintentional) to its long-term success. As it stands today, there is competition between prudent practices aimed at efficiently securing the retirement income of America's workforce, and non-fiduciary services created for business purposes of service providers.

Obstacles to a Clear Understanding

- Conflicting and/or ambiguous Governmental messages that confuse qualification rules under IRC §401(a) with rules of fiduciary prudence and process as defined by Department of Labor regulation, case law, and other regulatory pronouncements.
- "Exemptions" given to fiduciary and non-fiduciary firms or individuals to receive compensation from trust assets without being legally held to a strict fiduciary standard of conduct. In other words, non-fiduciary motives in 401(k) plans have created a non-fiduciary operating environment. (The "Merrill Exemption" is one example)[2]
- ERISA has imposed a federal fiduciary duty and responsibility on business executives and board directors who serve as "ERISA Fiduciaries" requiring them to act *exclusively* in the best interest of plan participants and beneficiaries. A growing chorus of benefit industry gurus believes that such executives and directors had a *pre-existing* fiduciary duty and responsibility to the owners of the business. Query: Has ERISA unintentionally imposed an incurable conflict of interest? That is, can any person faithfully serve the best interest of two conflicting masters? Plan participants may believe they are out of harm's way and protected, as fiduciary oversight is mandated by ERISA, but increasingly these fiduciaries appear to be like a sightless watchdog that doesn't bark.
- Fiduciary ignorance, fear, uncertainty, and doubt, which leads to non-fiduciary decisions and practices.

Identifying Non-Fiduciary Practices, and Their Associated Costs

Decisions and/or functions that are clearly fiduciary in nature include proactively monitoring costs, selecting a proper number of efficient investments necessary to construct an appropriate portfolio, and operating the plan in exact accordance to its purpose – which is to deliver retirement income to its beneficiaries.

Decisions and/or functions that are clearly imprudent include purchasing high cost investments and services when their identical match is available at perhaps less than half the cost, or turning a blind eye to obvious mishandling of trust assets by non-fiduciaries (i.e. the participants) and, at the same time, claiming for themselves protection from fiduciary liability under 404(c).

There are other decisions and/or functions that fall into a gray area. Such decisions or functions might be prudent, or they might not be.

The significance of this explanation is that some fees are obviously necessary and prudent. Some fees are hidden and imprudent and pay for excessive or unnecessary services. Finally, there are fees that could be improper in some plans, and acceptable in others, and it takes an experienced, discerning eye to recognize the differences.

Excessive is as Excessive Does

The following examples show the interplay between various imprudent, hidden, and excessive fees as influenced by the 401(k) culture described above.

Even at this time, a blatant non-fiduciary based feeding frenzy is taking place at the expense of American workers' 401(k) plans.

"The mutual fund industry is now the world's largest skimming operation - a $7 trillion (now$12 trillion) trough from which fund managers, brokers, and other insiders are steadily siphoning off an excessive slice of the nation's household, college, and retirement savings. "[3] *($12 trillion update added)*

Most experts agree that trust fiduciary laws are nominally default rules,[4] and hence should be simple to adhere to and operate under. However, managing 401(k) plans is anything but simple. It's a jumbled mess because non-fiduciary investment sales people have infiltrated, and now control what was intended to be a purely fiduciary function.

It would be simple to obtain optimal results. Then why isn't it happening?

For example, the S&P 500 Index consistently outperformed 98% of fund managers over the past three years, 97% over the past 10 years ending October 2004, and 94% over the past 30 years.[5]

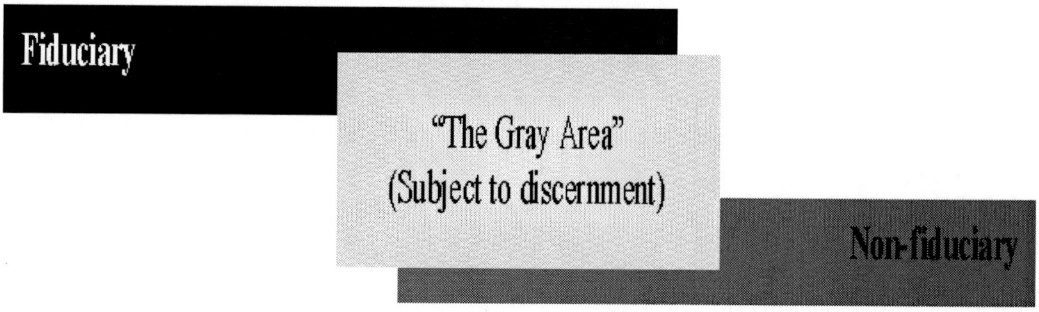

Recent studies reveal (and many more continue to substantiate), that a passive 60% stock, 40% bond portfolio outperformed 90% of the nation's largest corporate pension plan portfolios, "run by the world's best and brightest investment minds."[6] The average return on actively managed equity mutual funds over the past 35 years trails the S&P by 87 basis points per year, and 105 basis points on broader indexes. "Over long periods, this difference in return amounted to substantial differences in wealth."[7] This is an unnecessary waste of participant's hard earned money. "This is why most academic and many professional advisors recommend that the best investment strategy is to match the market's performance. You can do this by putting your money in a fund that holds all stocks in proportion to their market value. Since these index funds do no research and little trading, the costs of holding their portfolios are extremely small, some ranging as low as 0.10 percent a year."[8]

Then why do literally hundreds of thousands of 401(k) plan fiduciaries do just the opposite? It's because they are "guided" to particular decisions by non-fiduciaries (i.e. brokers, registered representatives, insurance agents, etc.) in pursuit of compensation which very frequently is in the form of hidden and excessive fees.

MAKING SENSE OF IT ALL

Following are some of the usual hidden costs found in 401(k) plans.

Hidden Costs #1 – Undisclosed Trading Costs

The assets held in account for the benefit of participants and beneficiaries do not belong to them. These assets are owned by an "entity," **which is the trust**. The participants are entitled to *future* benefits from the trust. This is an important concept in trust governance. In other words, if the investments belonged to the participants right now, there would be no need for fiduciaries. Therefore, the fiduciaries are charged with making decisions for the future benefit of others, based on what they deem appropriate for the participants and beneficiaries, in a similar way a member of the House of Representatives makes decisions for their constituents. The decision is based upon what they judge to be in their constituents' best interests.

*"The new prudent investor rule directs the trustee to invest based on risk and return objectives reasonably suited to the **trust**."*[9]

A major flaw in the 401(k) system, therefore, is allowing non-fiduciaries (in this instance, plan participants themselves) to control trust assets by choosing without skill from a large array of investment choices, carefully presented in such a way as to generate additional brokerage (trading) commissions by encouraging "active" trading within participant accounts. In other words, emotional reactions of participants who lack investment expertise trigger undisciplined and imprudent investment decisions in the trust, when a simple 60% stock, 40% bond portfolio described above is well within the reach of every single participant. The brokerage and investment fund industries not only fully understand that participants are making imprudent investment decisions, but are *counting on participant ignorance to generate revenue*. This is a substantial and hidden cost that participants are almost universally unaware, and have no concept of how it is reducing the future retirement income they would otherwise receive. The average actively traded mutual fund experiences approximately 80% turnover per year, meaning that 80% of the underlying stocks and/or bonds are sold each year. It is estimated that for every 1% in turnover, there is 1% in added brokerage commission cost. Hence, the average mutual fund has an added cost of .8% (otherwise known as 80 "basis points"). This is the first hidden and unnecessary cost.

It becomes easier to understand why so many 401(k) plans primarily offer (1) actively managed investment choices, and (2) more funds than are necessary to construct a prudent, low cost portfolio. It also demonstrates rampant ignorance that exists in the fiduciary ranks – in plans large and small.

*"TheStreet.com profiled a fund last year that had a 5 star rating, a 1% expense ratio, and **800 bps** in brokerage expense."*[10]

Reducing net returns through unnecessary and excessive brokerage expenses is a non-fiduciary and imprudent practice that runs counter to the principles set forth in ERISA, which is to secure the retirement of American workers. Consider the chaos that would result if Congress gave each citizen 15 laws to choose from. Individually, we might pick and choose those we deem appropriate for us and, in turn, adhere only to the particular laws we chose. The principle of fiduciary prudence is that fiduciaries make decisions for all individuals to whom they are responsible based upon what is in their best interest, whether they like it or not. As unpopular as this concept is, we must not equivocate on protecting participants and beneficiaries from their own lack of knowledge.

The current 401(k) culture has eroded the principles of true fiduciary governance through the begging, pleading, lobbying, or through other ways and means, fiduciaries collectively have drifted from "protecting their future retirement security" to "give them what they want whether it's good for them or not."

Hidden Costs #2– SEC Rule 28(e) "Soft Dollar" Revenue Sharing

SEC Rule 28(e) legalized charging "excess" brokerage commissions. 28(e) permits hidden cost #2 to exist, and is symbiotic with Hidden Cost #1 above. Rule 28(e) violates fundamental fiduciary rules by permitting plan assets to be used for purposes other than for the exclusive benefit of the participants and beneficiaries. 28(e) Soft Dollars are generated by active securities trading within mutual funds and similar investment vehicles. Allowing "Soft Dollars" to go un-captured and un-credited back to the 401(k) trust is not a fiduciary practice, and the historical problems caused by soft dollars are self evident.

It's important to take a moment to explain how 28(e) excess commissions came to be. Shortly after the creation of the IRA, but before the creation of the 401(k) as we know it, a change occurred within the brokerage and mutual fund industry. As part of the Securities Acts Amendments of May 1975 (SAA '75), fixed commission rates on the purchase and sale of securities through brokerage firms were eliminated. The significance of the elimination of fixed commission rates would prove to be one of several core issues of debate regarding fees in retirement plans. This would ultimately allow brokerage firms to charge excess commissions, thereby creating "at play" dollars that actually belonged to the participants, which is commonly referred to as "soft dollar" revenue or "SEC Rule 28(e)" excess commissions. With hundreds of billions of securities trades each year, the excess commissions made available by SAA '75 would forever change the investment and retirement plan industry. These soft dollars, coupled with the urgent need to compete in the 401(k) industry and the creation of the 12(b)-1 in 1980 created the "perfect fee storm," which until now has existed with little or no notice by Federal regulators, plan sponsors, participants, or the general public.

As a result of the Securities Acts Amendments of 1975, Section 2 8(e) was added to the Securities Exchange Act of 1934. With fixed commission rates no longer the law, Section 28(e) created a safe harbor for brokerage firms who exercise *no investment discretion* as defined under Section 3(a)(35) of the 1934 Act to be able to charge a fund a commission that was more than what it actually costs to execute, clear, and settle a securities transaction *without violating the law or fiduciary duties*. A brokerage firm may also choose not to operate within the safe harbor, further obscuring costs and making even more difficult for a fiduciary to fulfill their ERISA mandate to know and monitor fees, commissions, costs, expenses, etc.

"It can be difficult for all but the most sophisticated investors to understand and effectively monitor an adviser's use of soft dollars outside the safe harbor, and to understand their impact on the adviser's expenses and trading activity. Moreover, the 1998 OCIE (Office of Compliance Inspections and Examinations, U.S. Securities and Exchange Commission) Report noted that disclosure by advisers concerning their use of soft dollars was not very effective; less than half of the advisers examined provided disclosure 'with sufficient specificity to enable clients or prospective clients to understand what was being obtained.'Even more importantly, OCIE found that, of those advisers who purchased products or services outside the safe harbor, ***none*** *provided sufficient disclosure."*[11] (OCIE clarification added)

Failing to operate within the safe harbor such as charging excess commissions associated with products and services that were readily and customarily available and offered to the general public on a commercial basis[12] is not necessarily a violation of securities law, nor is it really the point. When qualified retirement plan assets are involved, the practice of charging excess commissions without the knowledge and understanding of the plan fiduciaries is most certainly a violation of the principles of fiduciary prudence and other ideals set forth by ERISA, and are an unnecessary expense borne by participants.

Excess commissions are used to purchase additional services from the brokerage firm in the form of presumably valuable investment research. In order to receive protection under the safe harbor, the fund manager must act in good faith to ensure the excess commission was "reasonable in relation to the value of brokerage and research services provided by the broker-dealer." Since excess commissions are subject to fiduciary jurisdiction, a fiduciary to the plan must be the one who determines whether excess commissions are reasonable and appropriate for participants to pay, not the fund manager receiving the "benefit" of the excess commissions. From a true fiduciary perspective, it is difficult to justify their existence considering a passive indexing approach requires no research and also consistently outperforms 90% of actively managed approaches that do require research. Considering this, a prudent fiduciary might question the value of such research. The 10% that do outperform an indexing approach statistically are temporarily fortuitous.[13] If you follow the money, modern investment research (in the context of this discussion) arguably exists so fund managers can benefit from 28(e) excess commissions, not to provide consistent market returns to participants.

Actively traded funds inherently have higher trading costs. In other words, every time a mutual fund manager buys and/or sells the underlying securities within the fund, the participants' return is decreased by the cost of those trades. Part of the reason for this lies in the fact that "excess" commissions are being charged for non-fiduciary purposes.

SEC rule 28(e) encourages turnover of underlying securities and the associated cost of trading because fund managers receive rebates of excess commissions from the brokerage firms for clearing the Funds' securities trades. This explains why the intelligent approach so widely accepted by the world's most astute investing minds is thrown out the window in 401(k) plans. Brokerage and Fund companies work together to generate excess commissions at the expense of participants, *because they believe they can indiscriminately do so*, not because it is prudent, intelligent, or advisable.

Prior to ERISA, fund managers used "excess" commissions generated from securities transactions to buy additional goods or services from their chosen brokerage firm. For example, if a trade costs 3.5 cents per share (trade execution, clearance and settlement), and the brokerage fixed commission was 5 cents per share, the excess 1.5 cents could either be used to purchase additional goods or services from the broker that directly benefited the account holder, or be credited back to their rightful owners, the account holders. Excess brokerage commissions (28(e) soft dollars) were handled the same way for IRAs and qualified plans.

After ERISA, the practice of using such soft dollars in IRAs would remain the same, but with respect to participants and beneficiaries within a qualified 401(k) plan subject to rules of fiduciary prudence, a conflict clearly exists with ERISA sections 403 (c)(1), 404(a)(1), 406(a)(1)(D), 406(b)(1) and 406(b)(3).

- ERISA 403(c)(1) states that the assets of a plan "shall never inure to the benefit of any employer and shall be held for the *exclusive* purposes of providing benefits to participants in the plan and their beneficiaries and defraying reasonable expenses of administering the plan." *Significance: Using soft dollars for purposes other than for the exclusive purpose of providing benefits to participants and beneficiaries and paying operational costs of the plan itself is a fiduciary breach.*

- ERISA 404(a)(1) states that a fiduciary must act prudently and solely in the interest of the participants and beneficiaries. *Significance: Using soft dollars to buy loyalty of brokerage firms, consultants or other parties-in-interest to the plan is a fiduciary breach.*
- ERISA 406(a)(1)(D) states that a fiduciary *shall not* transfer to, or use by or for the benefit of a party-in-interest, any assets of an ERISA governed plan. *Significance: Use of soft dollars could effectively be a transfer to a party-in interest, thereby creating a fiduciary breach.*

Due to the lack of oversight of 28(e) Soft Dollar Revenue in qualified retirement plans, the Securities and Exchange Commission was compelled to address the issue before the Congressional Subcommittee on Capital Markets, Insurance and Government Sponsored Enterprises, Committee on Financial Services. This occurred on June 18, 2003, shortly after H.R. 2420, the "Mutual Funds Integrity and Fee Transparency Act of 2003" was presented to the House of Representatives by Chairman Baker, Ranking Member Kanjorski and other members of the Subcommittee. According to the testimony of Paul F. Roye, Director, Division of Investment Management of the SEC, the Mutual Funds Integrity and Fee Transparency Act would:

- Provide investors with disclosures about "estimated" operating expenses incurred by shareholders, soft dollar arrangements, portfolio transaction costs, sales load break points, spreads, directed brokerage (a practice banned in mutual funds by SEC in 2004[14]), and revenue sharing arrangements.
- Provide investors with disclosure of information on how fund portfolio managers are compensated.
- Require fund advisers to submit annual reports to fund directors on directed brokerage and soft dollar arrangements, as well as on revenue sharing.
- Recognize fiduciary responsibility and obligations of fund directors to supervise these activities and assure that they are in the best interest of the fund and its shareholders.
- Require the SEC to conduct a study of soft dollar arrangements to assess conflicts of interest raised by these arrangements, and examine whether the statutory safe harbor in Section 28(e) of the Securities Exchange Act of 1934 should be reconsidered or modified.

While it is commendable that the SEC has decided to act on this issue, 17 years earlier the U.S. Department of Labor issued ERISA Technical Release 86-1 notifying the public of this very issue. The nature of ETR 86-1 was to "reflect the views of the Pension and Welfare Benefits Administration (PWBA) with regard to 'soft dollar' and directed commission arrangements pursuant to its responsibility to administer and enforce the provisions of Title I of the Employee Retirement Income Security Act of 1974 (ERISA)."

An excerpt from ETR 86-1 states:

"It has come to the attention of PWBA that ERISA fiduciaries may be involved in several types of 'soft-dollar' and directed commission arrangements which do not qualify for the 'safe harbor' provided by Section 28(e) of the 1934 Act. In some instances, investment managers direct a portion of a plan's securities trades through specific broker-dealers, who then apply a percentage of the brokerage commissions to pay for travel, hotel rooms and other goods and services for such investment managers which do not qualify as research with the meaning of Section 28(e). In other instances, plan sponsors who do not exercise investment discretion with respect to a plan direct the plan's securities trades to one or more broker-dealers in return for research, performance evaluation, and other administrative services or discounted commissions. The Commission (SEC) has indicated that the safe harbor of Section 28(e) is not available for directed brokerage transactions."

Directed brokerage arrangements between mutual fund managers and brokerages is now a banned practiced. Prior to its ban, fund managers would direct trades through brokerages' trading desks to reward the brokerage for selling their funds to retail clients. Notwithstanding the ban on directed brokerage, 2 8(e) excess commission arrangements not only still exist, but are very common.

SEC investigations have shown that "28(e)" excess commissions have been used by "non-fiduciary" consultants to make certain services available to mutual funds.

Among them:

- Conferences and other similar group meetings where the consultant invites both the "client" (i.e. a 401(k) plan sponsor/trustees) and representatives of the mutual funds who want to sell their funds to the client of the consultant. In other words, the mutual fund pays the consultant a significant amount of money to be invited to meetings where the consultant's clients will be in attendance.
- Sales and marketing support to the mutual fund's staff.
- "Objective looking" performance reports that paint the mutual fund in the best light, and facilitate the sale of that fund to clients of the consultant.
- Other "image enhancement" or "sales facilitation" services.
- Loyalty of consultant or brokerage firm.

Expensive and hidden 28(e) excess commission practices hurt plan participants and their beneficiaries, impede fiduciary oversight, and violate ERISA Sections 403(c)(1), 404(a)(1) and 406(a)(1)(D). 28(e) soft dollars are the most difficult fee to uncover. Like directed brokerage, the practice of charging excess 2 8(e) commissions should also be banned in all qualified retirement plans.

Hidden Costs #3 – Sub-Transfer Agent Revenue Sharing

The following is a rather lengthy, but important illustration of the widespread practice of subsidized record keeping services through excess mutual fund management fees.

Envision a meeting among three individuals. An employer with 75 employees, wanting to design a brand new plan for their employees; a Registered Investment Representative; and a Record Keeper commonly referred to as a "Third Party Administrator." After the meeting, the employer requests formal proposals from the Investment Representative and the Record Keeper. They leave the employer's office and agree to work together to design a plan that works for all parties. The Registered Representative and the Record Keeper collaborate and develop two proposals for the employer to consider.

The first proposal recommends 6 mutual funds, 4 of which are actively traded mutual funds. As a portion/component of the Funds' Management Fees, the 4 actively traded mutual funds pay a .5% "finders fee" of each new dollar invested to the Registered Representative plus a .5% trail commission - referred to as a 12(b)-1 commission. (A more detailed discussion of 12(b)-1 commission will be forthcoming later in this testimony). The Record Keeper proposes a $4,000 base fee per year, plus $60 per participant per year, paid by the employer.

When the employer does the math, he discovers that if each of his 75 employees contributed $100 per semi-monthly pay period, the Investment Representative would earn $100 x .5% x 75 x 24 = $900 the first year, and every year thereafter, plus an additional .5% on the accumulating balance. This $900 doesn't seem like much, especially when compared to the record keeping fee $8,500 ($4,000 base fee plus $4,500 (75 participants x $60)).

The employer looks at the record keeping fees, squirms a little, and quietly questions whether the record keeper's services are really worth $8,500 per year.

Summary of Proposal A

Cost Item	Investment	Record Keeping
Finders Fees	$900 per year	N/A
Ongoing Commissions	$900 and growing	N/A
Base Fees	N/A	$4,000
Per Head Charges	N/A	$4,500

Then he requests Proposal B. Having experienced that reaction before, the Investment Representative and the Record Keeper are prepared to present something more palatable.

The second proposal consists of 12 mutual funds, 9 of which are actively traded. To the employer's delight, proposal B seems much better. The Investment Representative's compensation remains the same, but the Record Keeping fee is cut by 70%! The base fee is reduced to $800 per year, and the per-head charge is reduced to $25.

Summary of Proposal B

Cost Item	Investment	Record Keeping
Finders Fees	$900 per year	N/A
Ongoing Commissions	$900 and growing	N/A
Base Fees	N/A	$800
Per Head Charges	N/A	$1,875

This proposal seemed like the best of both worlds. Twice as many mutual fund options for one-third the cost! The employer thinks participants will love it, and of course he loves it, too. It doesn't occur to the employer that he should question the economics, or whether there are fiduciary implications to going with one proposal vs. another. It seems like a no-brainer, so the decision is made to go with Proposal B.

Fast forward 10 years and the employer now has 150 employees, and $4 million dollars in the plan. As far as the employer is concerned, the economics are still the same as the first day the plan was adopted. However, there was an element the employer didn't understand. Remember the reaction to the $8,500 fee for record keeping fees? The employer wasn't certain if that was a fair fee for services rendered. Maybe it was fair, and if that was the case, the employer might have reduced or cut-back on various optional "elements" of the plan to arrive at a fee that seemed appropriate, all services considered.

Summary of costs 10 years later – Proposal B (the "believed–to-be" costs)

Cost Item	Investment	Record Keeping
Finders Fees	$1,800 per year	N/A
Ongoing Commissions	$20,000 growing	N/A
Base Fees	N/A	$800
Per Head Charges	N/A	$3,750

The $2,675 in fees associated with Proposal B seemed about right. With the growth of the company and the plan, the fact that plan costs also increased went without saying. Looking back at the original "deal", the employer computes the fees and costs as he thinks it stands today. All things remain the same except for 150 participants instead of 75, and there are $4 million dollars in assets.

Paying the record keeper $4,550 ($3,750 + $800 = $4,550) for such an extensive array of services rendered is perceived as being a little low. The employer intuitively knows the record keeper is worth more than $4,550, but is uncertain "how much more." If the record keeper needed more money for their services, they would certainly ask for it, and if they don't request more they must be satisfied. The employer also notices the Investment Representative is now being paid over $20,000 – and given all of the enrollment and investment education meetings – along with all of the reports, trustee meetings, and general education given to the fiduciaries, it might seem "about right."

Luckily for the employer and the participants, the employers' niece happened to be a student of fiduciary prudence and retirement plan economics and something seemed "fishy" to her.

After looking into the economics of "Proposal B" today, the employer's niece reluctantly brought the bad news. Something has gone terribly wrong, and the employer is stunned beyond words. Here's how the ***true*** economics look:

How could the record keeper be making more money than the Investment Representative? *Ten thousand dollars* more... and growing!

Remember the "collaboration" the Investment Representative and Record Keeper originally entered into? Proposal B involved the payment of Sub-Transfer Agent fees (Revenue Sharing from the Mutual Funds). The increase in funds was not an added benefit to the employer or employees as initially believed. Rather, it was a carefully calculated design element to capture a particular type of revenue sharing based upon two things: (1) The number of funds offered multiplied by (2) the number of participants with assets in those funds.

Cost Item	Investment	Record Keeping
Finders Fees	$1,800 per year	N/A
Ongoing Commissions	$20,000 growing	N/A
Base Fees	N/A	$800
Per Head Charges	N/A	$30,150

Assume in this case 8 of the 9 actively traded mutual funds are being utilized by participants. Also assume that the mutual funds each pay $22 per participant per year. The true economics are therefore 150 participants x $22 Sub-Transfer Agent Revenue Sharing x 8 Funds = $26,400. When the existing "per head" fee paid by the employer ($3,750) and the base fee ($800) are added to the Revenue Sharing number, the new total is $26,400 + $3,750 + $800 = $30,950.

The employer is angry for four reasons. First, he feels deceived because he didn't understand the true economics of the plan. Second, he feels his ability was impeded to prudently judge whether the services rendered were worth what the Record Keeper received in actual compensation. Third, he understands now that the "extra" funds had nothing to do with helping participants build a better portfolio. It had everything to do with multiplying the potential revenue sharing – and that has not helped the participants at all. Fourth, the realization that the employer has allowed assets to be improperly spent on services with skewed economics might place him squarely in the cross hairs of an effective litigator. The record keeper may very well have earned every obscure penny, but the issue here is about transparent business practices and it's also about determining whether the additional $25,000 the record keeper received was for services consistent with fiduciary objectives. Although imprudent due to its hidden nature, ironically the fee to the record keeper could be both reasonable, and excessive (vs. reasonable **or** excessive). Reasonable from the stand point of performing the work necessary to fulfill the expectations of their client, yet also excessive from a fiduciary prudence standpoint because services are being performed that have nothing to do with securing the future retirement income of the participants in the plan.

Such is the nature of hundreds of thousands of 401(k) and similar retirement plans across the United States even as you read this. Sub-transfer agent revenue sharing should be banned so that fiduciary based plan services are priced upon unimpeded economics principles.

What is a Sub-Transfer Agent? (and Sub Transfer Agent Revenue Sharing?)

A transfer agent is usually a bank or trust company (or the mutual fund itself) that executes, clears and settles a security buy or sell order, and maintains shareholder records (i.e. accounts for "title" of the ownership of the shares). When certain functions of the transfer agent are sub-contracted to a third party, that third party becomes a "sub-transfer agent." Within the context of this paper, a sub-transfer agent would be one of the following entities:

1. A third party administrator.
2. A bank or trust company performing recordkeeping services.
3. Some other entity tracking the number of shares held for the benefit of a specific participant within an individual account plan.

Payment to these parties for this sub-contracted service has come to be known as "Sub-Transfer Agent fees." Sub-Transfer agent fees exist solely to support the participant directed account culture in actively managed mutual funds.

Sub-transfer agent fees are generally paid as a flat dollar, per-participant, per fund. For example, many funds will pay a third party administrator $10 per participant, per fund. Other funds will pay a percentage of assets - such as 5 to 10 basis points. However, some funds pay up to $22 per participant, per fund or 35 basis points. The problems with sub-transfer agent fees is not how much is being paid to the service provider. Rather, the problem is being unaware who is receiving the payments, and whether or not the payments fairly represent the value of the service being rendered. The Department of Labor has made it very clear that a plan sponsor must understand the value and associated compensation of each individual servicing company, thereby making the cost of the parts more important than the cost of the whole.

An estimated 100 million shareholder accounts, or approximately 40 percent of all mutual funds, are in sub accounts at financial or record keeping intermediaries at this writing. Approximately $2 billion dollars per year is paid to third parties for sub- accounting services. There are potential costly and ERISA-violating problems inherent in omnibus accounts with underlying participant directed sub-accounts which are beyond the scope of this testimony.

Hidden Costs #4 – Non-Fiduciary Compensation (12(b)-1 commissions)

There are two types of 12(b)-1 fees:

1. Sales commission 12(b)-1 - paid to a registered representative for selling mutual funds for an individual or within a plan.
2. Servicing 12(b)-1 - paid to a person or entity who services an account after the sale.

SEC Rule 12(b)-1 was enacted in 1980. It is partially responsible for the proliferation of mutual funds in individual account plans. Again, referring to the mutual fund relationship with the distribution medium (sales force) of the brokerage firm, it creates a conflict of interest between the brokerage firm and the mutual fund, thereby rendering each unable to devote their loyalties to the plan participants. It permits mutual funds to increase their internal fund expense ratio by up to 1% in aggregate.

The combination of these two commissions may not exceed 1%. For example, the sales 12(b)-1 could be 50 basis points (.5%) and the service 12(b)-1 could also be 50 basis points.

It is common to refer to both sales and servicing revenue as "12(b)-1" fees, not differentiating between the two. More than half of all mutual funds have a 12(b)-1 feature. These commissions are disclosed in the prospectus, but very few plan sponsors understand their significance to the plan, the participants, and the trustees.

The 12(b)-1 commissions are a concern because non-fiduciary sales people carefully place products with high 12(b)-1 commissions within 401(k) plans without the full understanding of the plan sponsor or trustees. Conversely, a Fiduciary Investment Advisor would be obligated to disclose fees in writing, invoice the plan sponsor or plan for those stated fees, and credit any 12(b)-1 fees back to the trust. This clear difference in behavior and reporting shows the crisis that exists in the industry. Plan sponsors don't know there is a difference; mutual funds are simply mutual funds to them.

Another seldom considered 12(b)-1 issue is that of unfair subsidy disparity. Fee subsidy disparity is often referred to by the fiduciary community as the "Hidden Tax" paid by participants with larger than average account balances because 12(b)-1 commissions pay for non-fiduciary services.

Illustration

Let's compare two hypothetical plans, Plan "A" and Plan "B." Let's say each has $50 million in assets, both have identical mutual funds and service providers, each paying 3% (1.50% in trading costs, and 1.50% in fund management fees). Further, assume that 40% of the fund management fee pays for revenue sharing arrangements (brokers, record keepers, insurance agents, and others), and 60% is kept by the fund manager. Let's also say that Plan "A" has 500 employees and Plan "B" has 2,500 employees.

Are costs consistent for all employees as a percentage of their account balances? Yes, of course. But what are the real economics? Take a look at the following example of a comparison between two hypothetical plans:

In this example, the participants of Plan "A" are subsidizing the overhead of Plan "B."

Hidden Costs #5 – Variable Annuity Wrap Fees

A Variable Annuity is an investment contract between a plan and an insurance company where (normally) a series of ongoing deposits are made to accumulate resources sufficient to pay a future benefit. Variable Annuities can be sold by insurance agents who have little or no formal investment or fiduciary training. Variable Annuities are separate vehicles that invest in mutual funds – they are not mutual funds in and of themselves.

Variable annuities offer a variety of investment options that are typically mutual funds investing in stocks, bonds and cash. Gains on variable annuities are tax deferred whether held in a qualified trust or not, and there are costs associated with this "built-in" tax deferral. The fee associated with obtaining this tax-deferred benefit is an insurance component. Therefore, one must ask whether or not putting a variable annuity in an ERISA-governed vehicle is necessary, or even wise. In other words, you could buy a lower cost mutual fund using the inherent benefits of a 401(k) and still get the deferral of tax. Paying the insurance company for the tax deferral may not be prudent. Variable annuities generally have higher expenses than comparable mutual funds, and these fees are assessed in such a way that each component service is "wrapped up" into one aggregate fee. Accordingly, this aggregate fee is called a "wrap" fee. The wrap fee hides individual component fees and services, which are:

Fee/Cost element	Plan A	Plan B
Gross fund fees and commissions	$1,500,000 ($50,000,000 x 3%)	$1,500,000 ($50,000,000 x 3%)
Revenue sharing	$300,000 1.50% x 40% x $50,000,000)	$300,000 1.50% x 40% x $50,000,000)
Revenue Sharing borne by each participant	$300,000 ÷ 500 participants = **$600 per participant**	$300,000 ÷ 2500 participants = **$120 per participant**

- **Investment Management**: Management fees of the mutual fund that is contained within the variable annuity. (Note that trading costs are in addition to the investment management component, and are extremely difficult to discover in variable annuity contracts.)

- **Surrender Charges**: If withdrawals are made from a variable annuity within a certain period of time after units are purchased within the annuity, the insurance company will assess a surrender charge. The charge is used to reimburse the insurance company for the commission payments they paid to a broker or insurance agent upfront. The surrender charge usually starts out higher, and decreases over the length of the surrender period.

- **Mortality and Expense risk charge**: This charge is equal to a percentage of the account value, typically 1.25% per year over the investment management fees - but could be more or less depending on who is purchasing the annuity. Consider this in light of what has already been revealed here. The total Plan fees and commissions could easily exceed 4.00% when mortality and expense risk charges are added. (For example, a potential scenario could look like this: 1% brokerage and trading costs, 1% fund manager costs, .15% in administration fees,.75% in sales/distribution commissions, and 1.25% in mortality fees. Total –4.15%)

- **Administrative Fees**: The insurer may deduct charges to cover record-keeping and other administrative expenses. It is common to see fees of $25 or $30 per year, or a percentage of each participant's account value, typically in the range of an additional .15% per year.

- **Fees and Charges for Other Features**: Stepped up death benefit, a guaranteed minimum income benefit, long-term care insurance etc. These fees are stated in the annuity contract, and are actuarially computed based on age, health, etc., and hence differ from participant to participant.

- **Bonus Credits**: Some insurance companies offer bonus credits, which is a credit back to the account of percentage of each purchase - e.g. 3% of each deposit. These types of accounts often have higher expenses, and the expenses can be larger than the credit. Bonus credits are generally "purchased" with *higher surrender charges, longer surrender periods, higher mortality and expense risk charges.*

Hidden Costs #6 – Administrative "Pass Throughs"

An unfortunate and yet almost universally common in 401(k) plans is an expense borne by all participants for unnecessary services demanded by a vocal minority. A fiduciary is obligated to protect and treat all participants equally. It is a violation of ERISA's exclusive benefit rule that millions of participants unknowingly pay for the undisciplined urges of others to immediately wrest benefit from their retirement plans. Three examples are:

- Easy loans taken against a participant's vested balance
- Open brokerage options
- Investment "advice" services

While some may argue that these plan features are available to all participants equally, and are therefore a reasonable expense to the trust. However, we must not confuse matters of coverage and non-discrimination in benefits rights and features (pursuant to IRC §401(a)(4)) with fiduciary prudence. Plan assets should not be used to pay for services that all Participants do not collectively receive or benefit from plan assets. In hundreds of thousands of companies across the U.S. there are assertive individuals, who are the vocal minority, that want various bells and whistles in their 401(k), and the unsuspecting end up having to pay for it. This subtle violation of the exclusive benefit rule is rampant and costly. Plans with optional benefits that increase the overall cost of plan operation should be paid for by the individual users or by the plan sponsor, not by the plan. These amounts vary from plan-to-plan, but they can be substantial, especially if the fees are "translated" into an asset based charge that goes un-examined year after year.

Hidden Costs #7 – Non-Fiduciary Mish-Mash

To wrap up this discussion, it's important to highlight a few remaining hidden costs. The following is not an all-inclusive list, because there are dozens of variations to each of these items, and even a few other costs that are highly complex and difficult to explain. These are beyond the scope of this hearing, but might be examined as part of a subsequent hearing. Some of the remaining fees and costs employers of all sizes are struggling to grasp are:

- Share class variances based upon plan size. (i.e. high load share classes in large plans. Common share classes include A, B, C, R, etc.)[15]
- Shadow Index Funds. These are basically funds that closely track passive indexes, but have "actively managed" prices. In other words, they are overly priced index funds, some overpriced by 200% to 300%.
- Suspected Intra-Fund pricing discrimination. (Evidence that this practice is now coming to light, but this is so new that independent fiduciaries are still trying to grasp the full nature and extent of this particular is sue.)[16] This is where a mutual fund cuts "deals" with preferred investors, and increases fees to non-preferred clients so that the total fee balances out to what is disclosed in the prospectus. For example, a prospectus of a two hundred million dollar fund might state that the fund

management fee is 1% of assets. The fund manager then "discriminates" against clients 2 – 6 by cutting a deal with preferred Client 1 that reduces their fee by half.

Clients 2 through 6 are paying for the backroom "deal" between the fund manager and client 1, and will experience lower returns at the same time, a clear example of investment return and cost discrimination. Also, other suspected violations of fiduciary prudence are coming to light where the "deal" isn't with a preferred client, but with the Investment Representative. This has even more serious implications when proven to be true.

	Assets	**Actual Fee**
Client 1:	$100,000,000	.50%
Client 2:	20,000,000	1.10%
Client 3:	20,000,000	1.10%
Client 4:	20,000,000	1.10%
Client 5:	20,000,000	1.10%
Client 6:	20,000,000	1.10%
Total:	**$200,000,000**	**1.00%**

Expert fiduciaries are still trying to get their arms around this issue. It's such a startling revelation that independent fiduciaries don't want to believe it, and hence are trying to find other reasonable explanations for their findings, hoping it simply isn't so. However, the economics of 401(k) plans are so defiant, entrenched, and arrogant, that it might very well be happening more often than one would like to think. Like Andrew Fastow, the former CFO of the complex ENRON "special purpose entities," maybe the industry thought no one would ever figure it out.

There is more that can and should be shared with legislators about other activities in the final markets that adversely affect participants and beneficiaries. I hope this testimony provides sufficient background to assist in grasping the issues at hand and comprehending the necessity of diligently considering possible solutions.

Possible Solutions

- Require full disclosure of all financial service provider costs and expenses. Create stiff monetary sanctions for any person, entity, or institution to withhold information from named fiduciaries for any qualified plan. This would require full transparency of all service provider activities and costs. It would enable fiduciaries to better understand the basis for their decisions regarding plan operations and investments. With improved understanding, the retirement income security of millions of Americans would be enhanced.
- Require fiduciaries to itemize any and all fees and expenses extracted from plan assets at any level, including trading commissions, spreads, management fees, soft dollar arrangements, finders fees, transfer agent fees, and other expenses, and to disclose those directly to participants on the Summary Annual Report. This will

demonstrate to participants that fiduciaries are aware of the costs the plan is bearing, and that they are taking responsibility for those costs.

- Hold all individuals or companies who are paid from plan assets to a fiduciary standard. This includes brokers, insurance agents, record keepers, actuaries, and others. Those individuals or professionals unwilling to assume fiduciary responsibility could negotiate payments directly from plan sponsors.
- Require all investment vehicles held in a qualified trust (within the meaning of Internal Revenue Code §501(a) and ERISA §403(a)) to be "revenue sharing free" which would include barring 28(e) soft dollars, 12(b)-1 marketing or servicing commissions, and sub transfer agent fees. When fiduciaries are empowered with full and accurate information about how 401(k) plans really work, they will logically demand transparent pricing, and each service component will be viewed critically and individually and solely upon its own merits. Services not absolutely necessary for building and securing future retirement income will be difficult to justify through a prudent fiduciary lens. Knowledgeable and informed fiduciaries will then be able to confidently determine what fees and costs participants and beneficiaries should bear.
- Eliminate Department of Labor Regulation 404(c). Plan sponsors and service providers have hidden behind this regulatory allowance as a perceived shield from fiduciary liability while ignoring the plight of workers who desperately need guidance and oversight for their investments. Rule 404(c) is non-fiduciary at its core, and it encourages other decisions and behaviors that are not in the interests of securing the retirement incomes of American workers.

Conclusion

Thank you for the invitation to testify before this committee. It is my earnest belief that the workers of America deserve proper protections for the hard earned savings they have set aside in their 401(k) plans – protections which they are denied in the current state of the industry. I also believe that the problems with the industry can be solved rather simply, though it will require confronting powerful economic interests that support the current system. But America's workers deserve better than they have received to date from the providers of financial services. Finally, thank you for beginning the daunting task of tackling this very important and relevant social issue that will affect millions now and in the coming decades.

End Notes

[1] Investment Fiduciary, Randy "Bubba" Cloud, founder of CNMLLC. Accredited Investment Fiduciary Auditor and a member of the Revere Coalition, a non-profit fiduciary advocacy group of independent investment fiduciaries.

[2] http://registeredrep.com/news/sec-merrillrule-debate/

[3] Statement by Senate Governmental Affairs Subcommittee on Financial Management, The Budget, and International Security. November 3, 2003, Senator Peter G. Fitzgerald (R- IL)

[4] http://papers.ssrn.com/abstract id=868761

[5] http://www.ifa.com/Book/Book pdf/overview.pdf - "Step 5"

[6] Dimensional Fund Advisors, Basic 60/40 Balanced Strategy vs. Company Plans 1987-2003. FutureMetrics, 2004.

[7] http://finance.yahoo.com/expert/article/futureinvest/6953 - "The Truth About Money Management"

[8] Ibid – "The Birth of Indexing"

[9] http://papers.ssrn.com/abstract id=868761 page 2

[10] "Fee Forensics, The impact of brokerage expense and trade execution in mutual fund portfolios." 2005 Annual Conference of the Center for Fiduciary Studies. Santa Fe, New Mexico.

[11] http://www.sec.gov/rules/petitions/petn4-492.htm. OCIE Report, *supra* note 8, at 40. In addition, the Commission has, on a number of occasions, sanctioned advisers who have used soft dollars to pay for products and services outside the safe harbor without making adequate disclosure. *See, e.g.* , DawsonSamberg Capital Management, Inc., Investment Advisers Release No. 1889 (Aug. 3, 2000); Marvin & Palmer Assoc., Inc., Investment Advisers Release No. 1841 (Sept. 30, 1999); Renaissance Capital Advisors, Inc., Investment Advisers Act Release No. 1688 (Dec. 22, 1997).

[12] Securities Exchange Act Release No. 12251 (March 24, 1976) (the "1976 Release")

[13] http://www.efficientfrontier.com/cf/997/tough.htm

[14] Directed Brokerage Banned as of August 2004. However, the problem apparently still persists to an unknown degree. http://registeredrep.com/news/american-funds-charged, http://www.sec.gov/rules/final/ic26591.htm, http://www.ici.org/issues/mrkt/04 nasd dir brokerage final.html, http://findarticles.com/p/articles/mi hb3396/is 200412/ai n1 3131331, http://registeredrep.com/news/directed-brokerage-banned/

[15] http://www.nasd.com/InvestorInformation/InvestorAlerts/MutualFunds/UnderstandingMutualFundClasse s/ NASDW 006022

[16] A startling extract from an actual forensic fee audit performed by an investment fiduciary: "*We find it noteworthy that the funds in the Plan are paying out more than half of the revenue they receive for 'investment management'. In fact, one fund (fund name deleted) is paying out 150% of the revenue that it discloses by prospectus. Several other funds (mostly name deleted / name deleted funds) pay out more than 70% of their receipts. Obviously, this indicates that they may be making up their lost revenues in some other manner. We spot checked the SAIs of a couple of the Plan's funds and found hidden expenses in excess of .50%for transaction expenses. Some portion of this money goes back to the manager in one form or another (research services, commission rebates, etc.). We estimate that the true investment and recordkeeping cost of the plan is significantly greater than the .94% that is revealed by the basic plan expense ratios.*"

In: Impact of Financial Crisis on Retirement Security
Editor: John J. Turner
ISBN: 978-1-60692-960-5

Chapter 16

WRITTEN TESTIMONY OF STEPHEN J. BUTLER, PRESIDENT OF PENSION DYNAMICS CORPORATIONS, AUTHOR AND WEEKLY FINANCIAL COLUMNIST ON "UNDERMINING WORKER'S RETIREMENT SECURITY" PRESENTED TO THE COMMITTEE ON EDUCATION AND LABOR, U.S. HOUSE OF REPRESENTATIVES

Stephen J. Butler

A BRIEF HISTORY

The 401(k) phenomenon is an accident in legislative history that has changed the face of America's retirement system. Voluntary pre-tax contributions from employees have generated substantial financial resources that provide a comfortable retirement for many. Considering the average American employee, early projections indicated that these plans would generate roughly five times the asset value at retirement than would have been received from the continuation of what was then a combination of qualified profit sharing, money purchase and defined benefit plans. Current statistics for the average employee who has been a participant for at least twenty years (and who is in their early 60's) support this original projection. The $3 trillion now accumulated in 401(k) plans offers a testimonial to their success.

The fact that pension laws have evolved to provide what amount to "portable" pension plans is critical in a country where the average employee changes jobs every seven years. The Bureau of Labor Statistics recently determined that the average employee born between 1957 and 1964 has had 10.5 different jobs between ages 18 and 40. Twenty-one percent of this group have had 15 jobs. Only fifteen percent have had fewer than four jobs. Those with college degrees had no better statistics regarding job stability than those without degrees.

To the extent that the traditional retirement plan system (that which preceded the 401(k) era) failed to meet expectations, its failure was largely attributable to the practical reality of employee turnover. Traditional pension benefits were designed to create a form of "golden handcuffs" with vesting schedules that rewarded only those employees who remained with a company long enough to become vested in their retirement benefits. In the early '70's, this could have required as much as ten years of service. A direct quote from President Reagan at the time was that he wanted to create "portable pension programs." Over 70% of working Americans work for companies having less than 100 employees. A large percentage of these employees work for companies with less than 25 employees. In the past, small, relatively unstable companies rarely offered traditional retirement plans when employer contributions were the only source of funds. Today, many offer some variation of a 401(k) plan or the small-company equivalent in the form of SIMPLE 401(k)'s.

The complicated laws requiring 401(k) plans to pass non-discrimination tests has compelled company owners and highly-compensated managers to spend time and money promoting plans to all rank and file employees. Without substantial contribution percentages from these non-highly compensated people, the managers were limited to contribution amounts below the legal maximums. This has prompted management to do everything in their power to promote the plans. Matching contributions, company discretionary contributions, employee meetings, individual financial advice and careful selection of investments are all a part of this promotional effort leading to the success of these plans.

Cost to Participants in General

The costs to 401(k) participants struggling to save for retirement is a detriment that has marred what would otherwise have been the unqualified success of the 401(k) phenomenon. Excessive fees, just over the past twenty years, have reduced participant account balances by an average of 15%. On a projected basis, excessive fees charged to participants will have reduced retirement "nest-eggs" by 20% according to a wide variety of organizations conducting research on the subject.

Understanding the Fundamentals of 401(k) Costs

Fees taken from plan assets to pay for administration and/or money management are paid with funds that could otherwise be earning and compounding on a tax-deferred basis.

The "Magic of Compound Interest" works against employees to dramatically magnify the loss of these missing dollars. The business term for this condition is "opportunity cost" -- - the calculated cost in dollars of a lost opportunity.

Example:

The best illustration of the cost of excessive fees is to project a flow of 401(k) contributions over time at percentage returns that reflect the difference of 1% (a typical amount of an "excessive fee.") Choosing $10,000 as an employee contribution amount is reasonable considering that we are looking well into the future. The median income today is $71,000 and the average contribution amount is 6-7%. In many cases, both members of a married couple are contributing, so $10,000 per year is not unreasonable. The returns for the American stock market have averaged 10% per year over a long historical period.

For the 20-year period through the 1980's and 1990's, the stock market averaged a 16% rate of return. Looking at what might be higher underlying rates of return going forward, the opportunity cost of the missing 1% is much higher. By 2000, many employees in expensive plans who had been participating for twenty years effectively paid the following amounts in opportunity costs as a result of high fees during that 20-year period.

After twenty years, this illustrates the actual cost for what might have been a single employee contributing $10,000 a year (or two people contributing $5,000 each) in the twenty years ending in 2000. Multiply these single-participant detrimental effects times the $3 trillion now in 401(k) plans and we can understand why the fee issue is critical.

Stop and recall for a moment the "Rule of 72" which states that money earning 7.2% doubles every ten years, and money earning 10% doubles every 7.2 years. Today's $3 trillion can be reasonably expected to double twice to $12 trillion in the next 14 years, thanks to reasonable investment returns and annual contributions. Excessive, undisclosed fees scheduled to cost participants as much as $2 trillion dollars is the problem we are here to try to correct.

Where the Abuse Begins

The greatest abuses are seen in the small-company environment where the average company owner is not a mutual fund or retirement plan expert. Large companies, by comparison, have reasonably sophisticated decision-makers. Xerox, for example, operated its own mutual funds and charged participants just 3/100ths of one percent per year. Participants in many small-company plans can be paying as much as 3 full percentage points --- exactly 100 times more for the same level of services.

The Opportunity Cost of a 1% Excess Cost - $10,000 Annual Contribution Percentage

Percentage Annual Return	Account Value 10 Years	Account Value 20 Years	Account Value 30 Years
10%	171,178	641,491	1,925,836
9%	162,568	566,549	1,570,441
Cost of 1% fee	8,610	74,942	355,395

The Opportunity Cost of a 1% Excess Cost - $10,000 Annual Contribution Percentage

Percentage Annual Return	Account value 10 Years	Account Value 20 Years	Account Value 30 Years
15%	232,057	1,279,641	6,008,782
14%	215,656	1,079,734	4,541,874
Cost of 1% fee	16,401	199,907	1,466,908

Technically, all fees charged to participants are disclosed today to plan sponsor decision-makers, but not all fees are disclosed to participants. In the insurance industry, for example, the practice of non-disclosure was justified by the rationale that "fees didn't matter --- net investment results were all that participants needed to see." This was an actual quote from the marketing Vice President of a major insurance company when interviewed by MONEY magazine in 1998.

Fees charged to participants may be stated in the investment materials, but they remain effectively hidden on an ongoing basis because participants never receive a bill and never see a separate line item outlining what their costs, in dollars, have been.

According to FORBES magazine, the mutual fund industry is the world's most profitable as it earns a consistent 30% pre-tax profit. Investors are not fee sensitive because they are focused on returns. Generally this means "chasing last year's best performing mutual funds."

In today's seamless electronic financial services arena, the hard-dollar cost of administering a mutual fund with at least $50,000 is 6/100ths of one percent per year—approximately $30. Virtually all 401(k) plans are administered in pooled accounts where the investor is the plan itself --- not the individual employee. As a result, virtually all 401(k) accounts, on a fund-by-fund basis, meet this $50,000 benchmark, meaning that the profit on the account is anything beyond the 6/100ths being charged. If the average mutual fund charge in a 401(k) investment is 1 full percentage point per year, the profit on those accounts might be as high as 94%.

In all discussions regarding fees, we have to take as a given that no single mutual fund or fund family can show that that they have consistently earned a higher rate of return (to justify higher fees) for any sustained length of time. The money management industry is a "zero sum game" in which all players revert to the norm at some point. Moreover, even when we can review past performance, there is no way to know prospectively whose performance might compensate for an excessive fee going forward. Over longer periods of time, a difference in performance among funds of the same type can be largely attributed to the difference in their costs to investors.

How 401(k) Plans Are Structured

Most 401(k) money is maintained today in a "daily-valued" electronic environment managed by the mutual fund or insurance companies themselves or the transfer agent industry that services the mutual fund industry. Plan participants can dial up their account information on an 800 voice-response number, but by far the most popular access is through the Internet. The raw cost of providing this seamless, electronic recordkeeping function is approximately $50 per year per participant. This is referred to as the "recordkeeping fee." It is the cost of maintaining the accounting of the participant's account.

Apart from the money management, there is the cost of complying with the layers of retirement plan regulations dictated by ERISA. This work is concentrated immediately after the end of every year when the discrimination testing must be completed. Later in the year, the government reporting form (Form 5500) for the plan must be completed and submitted. It is essentially a balance sheet and income statement for the plan. The cost of this compliance testing and administration is typically about $35-$60 per participant with a base company fee of $1,000- $1,500.

An Illustration of Fees in a Typical Plan

We can use an example a plan with 50 participants and $3,000,000 in assets. This is typical of an engineering or professional firm that has had a plan for twenty years. The record keeping and compliance cost for these 50 employees should be roughly $130 per employee. If the true cost of money management is only 6/100ths of a percent, the money management cost for $3,000,000 would be $1,800. The total cost of the plan would be $7,800. By comparison, a typical vendor in the industry today would be charging an average of $36,500 for this plan. Some have scheduled fees that would amount to as much as $60,000 or 2% of assets.

While a plan sponsor (the company) might be happy to pay for the administration cost, it will never pay total fees of this magnitude. Asset-based money management fees will always be charged to participants where they will be largely ignored. After all, no participant ever receives a bill or writes a check for these costs. They are automatically deducted from what would have been earnings --- or from principal in years when earnings may be negative.

Techniques That Obscure the Magnitude of Fees.

Having established that hidden excessive costs are a guaranteed detriment to optimizing savings results over time, it is generally easy to identify them when we know where to look. Some of the more difficult hidden costs, however, are those that are buried in the process and that will never show up in any stated cost to participants.

Non-disclosure at Participant Level in "Bundled Plans"

In the 401(k) marketplace, participants are told the annual expense ratios of the mutual funds offered by the plan, but administrative fees charged to their accounts are typically disclosed only in an annuity contract signed by the plan sponsor. This percentage amount is referred to as the "wrap fee" and it is typically one or two percent in a small company environment. The insurance industry is not legislated by federal laws, so the normal disclosure requirements demanded of the fund industry do not apply to insurance companies legislated only by state governments. In the mutual fund industry, the cost of administration, if presented as being "free," is usually imbedded in the expense ratios of the funds. Comparable funds, if not priced to support administration, could generally be found that would be less expensive for participants.

These plans that combine investment products with administration all provided by one company are referred to as "bundled" plans, and the providers of such plans are suggesting that "bundled" plans be exempt from any disclosure requirement to come out of these hearings. With what I estimate to be 70% of all 401(k) plans provided in this "bundled" format, making them exempt would emasculate any new disclosure requirements.

MUTUAL FUND INDUSTRY --- PROPRIETARY FUND REQUIREMENT

In the mutual fund industry, the fees to participants are disclosed because they are the normal annual expense ratios of the funds. They are spelled out in the prospectus of each fund and today are universally summarized in the employee promotional literature. The mutual fund industry does not add a wrap fee. Instead, a company such as Fidelity will insist that at least half of the funds selected for the plan include their own proprietary funds. Remembering that the profit from a 401(k) account can be as much as 94% to the fund family, the insistence that at least half of the funds come from the fund family's proprietary list ensures that the plan will be profitable. A refinement of this technique is to require that the so-called "core funds" will be proprietary. These are the large- company or balanced funds that traditionally attract as much as 70% of the money in the plan. So, while the fund requirement based on the number of funds may only be half of the offerings, the percentage of employee money in those funds can easily be 70% or more.

The balance of the funds offered in the plan may come from other fund companies as part of an effort to create a "veneer of objectivity" for marketing reasons. These other fund families will typically be limited to just those funds that charge enough to pay the primary fund family 25/100ths of one percent and possibly some additional funds to buy "shelf space" on the "platform" offered by the primary fund family selling and administering the plan.

What does this practice cost the participant? No single fund family offers superior funds across the entire spectrum of the industry. Common sense would tell us that selecting from a vast universe of choices will generate better fund selection than a limited universe from just a single fund family. Here, we are selecting funds for the convenience and pricing demands of the vendor --- not with the sole purpose of improving the outcome for the participant. Knowing that this is the case explains why major mutual fund companies in the 401(k) industry refuse to be construed as fiduciaries of the plan. Selling their own funds would be a prohibited transaction and would violate the requirement that fiduciaries make decisions based upon the "sole interests of participants."

In the sample plan above, (50 employees and $3,000,000) most vendors today would offer to do the administration and record keeping at no cost to the plan sponsor. A quick review of the arithmetic would explain why. Those administrative costs would have been about $7,000 and the plan is charging participants $30,000.

BARRING THE EXIT --- BACK-END CHARGES FOR PLAN SPONSORS WHO WANT TO LEAVE

The most egregious examples of excessive fees today are found in plans that are using share classes or annuity products that pay commissions up front and then have high ongoing fees to participants to offset, over time, the commission that was paid up-front. If a plan sponsor chooses to leave one of these plans there will be a "contingent deferred sales charge" otherwise known as a "back-end load." Eventually, the load grades down and disappears after five to seven years, but in the meantime, the plan sponsor can not leave without subjecting participants to an exit charge that can be as high as 5% of their assets. Moreover, the law specifically bars a plan sponsor from paying that cost as a company expense, because plan contributions can only be made as a percent of compensation --- never as a percent of assets. These are the plans that can be charging participants as much as 3% per year. Once introduced, they are locked in by exit charges for at least five years.

The insurance industry and the subset of the mutual fund industry selling through the NASD brokerage industry are selling these 401(k) packages with back-end loads. The pure no-load sub-set of the fund industry does not offer this format. The back-end-load phenomenon occurs only in an environment where a mutual fund sales person or insurance agent requires a sales commission that has to be charged to the plan.

FUNDS AS A "FEEDING TROUGH" FOR THE BROKERAGE INDUSTRY

As yet another example of a hidden fee, FORBES magazine published an article entitled, " What's the Matter With Brokers' Funds?" The fact that these funds generate relatively poor performance is well-established, and the reasons have to do with two facts. The article stated that ". .the whole psyche of a brokerage firm is built around selling, not buying. .Analysts at wire houses get ahead by helping underwriters, not by being skeptical." This is essentially saying that the brokerage-sponsored funds are used as a resource for investing in the kind of companies that the firm was underwriting. High turnover of assets in the funds also generated trading fees for the brokerage firm. I was once told by a Prudential-Bache retirement plan representative offering a "free" plan to a plan sponsor that "once we have the assets, we don't have to worry about making money." The FORBES article went on to say, "Another problem is that broker- sponsored funds tend to have steep expense ratios."

HOW AN EXPENSIVE PLAN CAN BE MARKETED

Thanks to the benefit of hindsight, a classic marketing ploy involves a presentation of funds from a new vendor candidate that have substantially out-performed the incumbent selection of the existing vendor. The current vendor, of course, is saddled with a selection of funds that were chosen three years previously in most cases. There are the problems of logistics and inertia that stand in the way of making changes in plans unless performance has fallen off a cliff. Of course, in this environment, a new set of fund choices will always look substantially better. The average plan sponsor rarely thinks to ask for examples of what the proposed new vendor's investment selections might be for a plan that they have operated for three years. There would typically be no improvement shown by this comparison.

This is symptomatic of how the consultants and marketing personnel in the industry can appear to be offering improvement when, in fact, they are simply rearranging the deck chairs and adding to the level of hidden fees in many cases. Representations of superior performance are a major tool used to take the focus away from participant fees.

Misinformed Decision-making on the part of Plan Sponsors

Section 404(c) is a U.S. Department of Labor regulation establishing requirements for plan sponsors that reduces their liability for making poor decisions with regard to the plan. Employees must be able to change investments and receive statements at least quarterly. They must be offered three basic fund types including a money market or guaranteed fixed income option. Finally, the plan must have a written investment policy statement, and employees should be provided with investment education (the latter being undefined and unspecified.)

Ironically, Section 404(c) proved to be a solution looking for a problem which then created a far more serious disadvantage for the employee participant. Since 1980 or the earliest days of the 401(k) phenomenon, virtually all plans offered quarterly statements and investment changes and a selection of different investment types. Remember that senior executives were major beneficiaries of these plans and they were inclined to want investment quality and flexibility. Virtually all plans operated under what was essentially an investment policy statement because decision-makers wanted decent investment choices for themselves.

The financial services community seized on Section 404(c) as the reason for hiring them to monitor the plan and therefore reduce liability. In fact, there was no practical liability for reasons having to do with 404(c). At industry conferences, lawyers were quick to point out that there were no lawsuits anywhere in the country brought by employees or groups of employees offered a selection of name-brand mutual funds and a rudimentary investment education and plan promotional effort.

The law of unintended consequences quickly created a "create the need" opportunity for the financial services community. An army of qualified and experienced "advisors" fanned out across the 401(k) Plan Sponsor community and talked about the potential liability of not using professional help and advice with regard to operating the plan. What this universe of advisors did not point out was that a.) there was no practical legal problem stemming from the way plans were typically being operated, and b.) the cost of this advisory service was going to be, at a minimum, one half percent to one full percentage point charged to plan participants---a cost that guaranteed a loss of up to 20% of retirement assets for each participant.

Meanwhile, there have been some lawsuits successfully filed against plan sponsors. The first that I am aware of was against First Union Bank settled for $25 million in behalf of the bank's employees. The bank was operating a collection of mutual funds, (Evergreen Funds which they owned at the time) and these funds were charging bank employees substantially more than 401(k) investments the bank was selling to its bank customers.

In the same vein, the recent class action suits against Fortune 500 companies such as Caterpillar, Boeing, Kraft and International Paper are all centered on fees --- not a lack of reporting, investment choice or investment education.

Avoiding Compliance Responsibility

While the financial services industry has seized upon Section 404 (c) and the scare tactics it can foster, they have deliberately avoided responsibility for most of the other IRS and Labor Department Regulations that they should be upholding when representing themselves as providing 401(k) administrative services. A typical service contract will have hold harmless language such as "the design and ongoing operation of your retirement plan needs to be reviewed by your tax and legal advisors." The "bundled provider" contract of one of the nation's largest mutual fund companies says the company will perform the 401(k) test and coverage test, but all other tests are the responsibility of the plan sponsor. In effect, the financial services industry is saying that they will do the work, but they are not offering a guarantee that it will be done correctly or completely. A plan failing an audit can cost the plan sponsor a substantial amount of money in legal fees and corrective measures. In an indirect way, this misrepresentation could be construed to be a hidden fee. The average plan sponsor assumes that the major financial institution handling their plan has taken responsibility for its compliance with all government regulations. In my experience, however, the immediate response when compliance problems arise is the voice on the phone saying, "read your contract."

THE SEARCH FOR A SOLUTION

To identify a solution, a process would involve working back from a perfect, if admittedly impractical, model.

Ideally, the best 401(k) plan would be one that charged nothing to the plan. All fees, even those associated with managing the mutual fund, would be charged to the company and paid with tax-deductible corporate dollars. A typical employee would be better off electing to have his or her taxable salary reduced slightly to help defray all or a portion of these costs. This would be far better than having the same costs deducted from plan assets that could be compounding on a tax-deferred basis.

Here's an actual example of that positive arithmetic. Over 800 dentists use a money management firm to manage retirement assets at their respective practices. The firm charges 1% of assets and routinely levies this charge against plan assets. In one actual case, I pointed out to a dentist that the firm was free to bill his practice for what, in this case was \$15,000 per year on \$1.5 million of assets. The net cost to the dentist billed directly, considering his 50% marginal state and federal tax bracket was \$7,500. Instead, the dentist was paying that year's \$15,000 with money in his plan that in 7.2 years (at a 10% annual return) would have doubled to \$30,000. In 14.4 years, it would have doubled again to \$60,000 --- in 22 years, \$120,000 etc. Obviously, the dentist asked to be billed directly and then started wondering if 1% might be little high for mediocre investment management that failed to beat basic benchmarks. The financial services industry will always opt to bill the plan directly because they do not want fees to become an issue. The arrangement outlined above had persisted for over twenty years. The billing format had a projected cost for the dentist and his employees of well over one million dollars of opportunity cost--- a cost that was reduced to a fraction of that amount in future years with the stroke of a pen.

Xerox charged just 3/100ths of one percent to its employees. Vanguard, on large amounts of money, can charge as little as 6/100ths of a percent and still make a profit. DFA is yet another mutual fund company renowned for its Vanguard-equivalent low fees. These organizations offer mute testimony to the fact that it doesn't have to cost what most of the industry charges to invest pools of money. An oligopolistic situation exists thanks to buyers who are unaware of the impact of fees. With few exceptions, nobody in the financial services industry wants to see this condition change.

THE SOLUTION

A simple but impractical solution would be to bar any organization that manages money from actually selling and administering 401(k) plans. The industry selling plans would be barred from receiving any revenue-sharing from the money management (mutual fund) industry. This would end the hidden fee elements seen in the brokerage industry and mutual fund industry where the sale of 401(k) plans is an engine for selling proprietary funds and generating trading commissions. There are 3,500 third party administrators across the country today who are independent of major financial institutions and that perform recordkeeping services and compliance work for retirement plans. Some of these companies, such as Hewitt Associates and Milliman and Roberts, are substantial and equipped to handle the nation's largest plans. Without this separation between product producers and 401(k) administration and sales, it is difficult to see how some of the more subtle examples of hidden costs can be avoided. Considering the foothold that mutual fund companies have in the industry, however, it is difficult to envision this as a practical solution. The horse is out of the barn.

The next option would be to have a national standard fee disclosure form required of any 401(k) presentation and require that it be renewed to reflect any change in investment mix. This standard would require that the cost in dollars and compound earnings over ten and twenty year time periods would be based upon the average fee charged to participants, assuming an even mix of investments across the entire spectrum of fund offerings. This would be stated on the front page of the 401(k) presentation and as part of the Summary Plan Description. In other words, a 401(k) vendor would have to show what the average opportunity cost would amount to over ten and twenty years based upon the average fee charged to a $10,000 per year contribution. It would be reasonable to assume a 10% rate of return as the starting point or gross return on investments assuming no fee. Fees would then be subtracted from this percentage amount, and the compound results would be illustrated. Using an average contribution of $10,000 per year would be simple (and inspirational.)

This comparison would illustrate the dramatic difference in costs over time between different vendors. It would offer a reality check for the average decision-maker who might otherwise have chosen a hidden-cost but expensive plan for his or her company. It is critical to require that the comparison use an example in dollars as I have suggested. To just require a stated percentage cost is too abstract. Even investment professionals have a hard time grasping the magnitude of opportunity cost presented by just a fraction of a percent in excess costs.

THE OUTCOME AND BENEFIT TO THOSE SAVING FOR RETIREMENT

Saving fees increases retirement benefits, in the aggregate, by as much as 15%-20%. How can this not be important enough to enact disclosure standards demanded of every company in the industry? Decision-makers may still purchase expensive plans for their employees, but not without hearing from the "self-styled mutual fund experts" that manage to find a voice in every company. An army of retirement savers have now deposited $3 trillion in their 401(k) plans. They are rapidly becoming a nation of reasonably sophisticated investors. For the most part, they know how to diversify investments, and they have lived through the volatility of stock market performance. This is a clear case where the glass is half full. The financial services industry can be commended for getting us this far. Going forward, however, we can improve results by insisting on an educational tool (comprehensive cost disclosure) that the industry acting on its own is inclined to avoid.

Stephen J. Butler is the founder and President of Pension Dynamics Corporation, a third party administration firm designing, installing, administering and advising 401(k) plans since 1980. He has written two books, "The Decision-maker's Guide to 401(k) Plans" and "401(k) Today." For the Knight Ridder newspapers, he has been a weekly columnist on retirement financial issues for seven years. He has been the author of articles and editorials in such publications as the Wall Street Journal, CFO Magazine and he wrote a cover article in MONEY entitled "Beware, Retirement Plan Rip-off." The latter article was an eight-page treatise on participant costs centered around the "Butler Index" which was the first published index of total costs paid for 401(k) services. He assisted the U.S. Department of Labor regarding their publication entitled, "Understanding Retirement Plan Fees and Expenses." Mr. Butler is a graduate of Harvard College, class of 1966, and attended the U. C. Berkeley Graduate School of Business Administration from 1966-1968. He is a Registered Investment Advisor, and he holds a Series 24 NASD license.

In: Impact of Financial Crisis on Retirement Security
Editor: John J. Turner
ISBN: 978-1-60692-960-5

Chapter 17

The 401(k) Fair Disclosure for Retirement Security Act - Myths v. Facts

John J. Turner

Myth: Too much disclosure will confuse 401(k) participants.

Fact: H.R. 3185 would require service providers to disclose their fees in terms that are clear and easily understandable, so that plan participants can make sound investment decisions for themselves. The biggest problem facing workers with 401(k) plans is that there is too little disclosure of fees, not too much. Plan participants should be presented with the facts and then allowed to make their own decisions.

Myth: Fees on 401(k)s are already adequately disclosed.

Fact: There is no one place that 401(k) plan participants can go to find out about the fees they are paying. Information that is available is difficult to find and difficult to read. And some fees are simply not disclosed *at all*. As a result, a 2007 survey by the AARP found that roughly 80 percent of plan participants were not aware of fees they were paying on their 401(k)s.

Myth: More fee disclosure will dramatically increase costs to plan participants.

Fact: Most experts agree that while there may be a small initial cost involved with disclosing the fees that participants are charged, continuing to hide fees puts Americans' retirement security at risk. It is reasonable that large financial services firms should have to tell their customers how much they charge for their services. And giving the investing consumer better information will encourage greater competition among financial service providers and help reduce fees.

Myth: Actively managed investments provide better returns than index funds.

Fact: Over the full twenty-year time period from 1983 to 2003, depending on the sector, index funds outperformed 89 percent to 97 percent of mutual funds. Index funds are not actively managed and therefore carry lower costs. While many 401(k) plans have made strides to include lower cost retirement options, index funds are still not available to workers in 30 percent of 401(k) plans.

Myth: Service providers that "bundle" their services will be required to unbundle them.

Fact: H.R. 3185 does not require service providers to unbundle their services. If a service provider sells investment management services, administrative services, and record-keeping together as a package, it may continue to do so. H.R. 3185 simply requires service providers to disclose the costs of the components of its bundled products.

Myth: H.R. 3185 mandates one investment option for every 401(k) plan.

Fact: H.R. 3185 would simply require all 401(k) plans to offer at least one index fund. It does not limit other types of investment options that 401(k) plans may offer; it does not tell 401(k) plans which specific index funds they must offer; and it does not require plan participants to invest in index funds. It simply ensures that participants are able to invest in an index fund if they choose to do so.

Prepared by the House Education and Labor Committee • April 2008 • http://edlabor.house.gov

INDEX

A

accountability, 97
accounting, 19, 48, 75, 81, 115, 126
actuarial methods, 76
adjustment, 78
administrators, 12, 21, 132
advertising, 71
advocacy, 120
age, 4, 8, 15, 34, 35, 36, 37, 41, 43, 50, 53, 66, 69, 76, 77, 82, 83, 84, 85,86, 87, 90, 117
ageing, 71
ageing population, 71
Alaska, 67
alternatives, 12, 19, 75
AM, 61
anxiety, 43, 65, 66, 93
arithmetic, 128, 131
ash, 45
assessment, 59
assets, 2, 3, 4, 5, 6, 7, 9, 10, 11, 12, 14, 15, 19, 21, 22, 28, 33, 34, 35, 36, 37, 41, 43, 46, 53, 55, 57, 59, 65, 66, 67, 71, 72, 73, 74, 75, 76, 77, 82, 84, 85, 90, 91, 94, 102, 103, 104, 105, 106, 107, 108, 109, 110, 113, 114, 115, 116, 118, 119, 120, 124, 127, 129, 130, 131
auditing, 3
authority, 4, 12, 15
aversion, 25, 29
avoidance, 60

B

BA, 61
baby boomers, 69
background, 119
bail, 26
balance sheet, 31, 126
banking, 4
bankruptcy, 45, 46, 55
banks, 4, 15, 48, 73, 90
basis points, 86, 106, 107, 115
behavior, 25, 34, 72, 82, 116
benchmarks, 131
bias, 66
bondholders, 46
bonds, 15, 28, 33, 34, 36, 45, 46, 65, 74, 107, 116
bone, 88
borrowers, 46
breakdown, 20, 32, 49
Budget Committee, 74
buffer, 34
business cycle, 60, 67

C

Canada, 70
candidates, 29, 68
case law, 104
cash flow, 57
cast, 31
CBS, 53

chaos, 107
children, 87
classes, 21, 86, 118, 128
clients, 40, 42, 89, 108, 111, 118
cohort, 83, 84
collaboration, 113
common sense, 101
community, 116, 130
compensation, 12, 13, 14, 17, 20, 39, 104, 106, 112, 114, 115, 129
competition, 104, 135
competitors, 34
complexity, 18, 43
compliance, 126, 127, 131, 132
components, 136
composition, 75
computing, 75
concrete, 88
confidence, 52, 73, 94
conflict, 12, 104, 109, 115
conflict of interest, 12, 104, 115
Congress, vi, 14, 17, 26, 28, 37, 48, 49, 53, 54, 60, 65, 66, 67, 68, 69, 71, 74, 90, 91, 95, 97, 99, 107
Congressional Budget Office, 60, 61, 74, 76, 78, 93
construction, 85
consultants, 2, 3, 12, 13, 72, 110, 111, 129
consulting, 7, 39
consumer price index, 15
control, 4, 15, 21, 104, 105, 107
corporate sector, 31
correlation, 41, 71
cost of living, 87, 88
cost saving, 60
costs, 11, 19, 21, 52, 53, 55, 57, 58, 59, 88, 98, 101, 102, 105, 106, 108, 109, 110, 113, 116, 117, 118, 119, 120, 124, 126, 127, 128, 131, 132, 133, 135, 136
counseling, 41
couples, 103
covering, 7, 52, 68
credit, 42, 45, 74, 116, 117
creditors, 41
criticism, 36
CRR, 62
culture, 41, 73, 101, 103, 105, 107, 111, 114, 115
cumulative percentage, 83
currency, 79
customers, 130, 135
CW, 62

D

danger, 90
database, 82
DCA, 93
death, 4, 51, 53, 117
debt, 35, 46, 67, 73, 79
decision makers, 4
decisions, 2, 3, 7, 11, 14, 15, 54, 60, 77, 103, 104, 105, 106, 107, 119, 120, 128, 130, 135
defined benefit pension, 66, 69
defined-contribution plans, 33, 34, 54, 74, 75, 77
definition, 81
delivery, 89, 101
demographic characteristics, 50
demographics, 49, 85
dentist, 131
Department of Commerce, 79
deposits, 54, 116
deregulation, 97
directors, 104, 110
disability, 51, 53, 58
disbursement, 69
discipline, 39, 59, 69, 104
disclosure, x, 2, 3, 8, 10, 13, 17, 20, 21, 22, 39, 108, 110, 119, 120, 121, 126, 127, 132, 135
discomfort, 52
discounting, 74
discrimination, 118, 119, 124, 126
disposable income, 51
distress, 49
distribution, 15, 33, 42, 50, 58, 72, 75, 77, 84, 115, 117
diversification, 27, 59, 60, 77
DJ, 61

Dow Jones Industrial Average, 22
draft, 14, 61, 71
drugs, 102
duties, 18, 22, 28, 103, 108

E

earnings, 8, 34, 37, 50, 57, 70, 72, 76, 77, 83, 102, 127, 132
cating, 94
economic activity, 67, 70
economic crisis, 88
economic downturn, 82
economic policy, 95
economics, 25, 113, 114, 116, 119
economies of scale, 9, 60
Education, vii, viii, x, 17, 25, 31, 37, 42, 43, 47, 65, 73, 79, 81, 87, 89, 93, 97, 101, 123, 135, 136
educational services, 42
egg, 87
elderly, 35, 76, 77
election, 53
elementary school, 87
email, 40
emotional reactions, 107
employees, ix, 1, 3, 15, 17, 18, 26, 27, 28, 40, 41, 42, 50, 53, 54, 55, 56, 58, 63, 71, 72, 76, 81, 82, 83, 84, 90, 102, 112, 113, 114, 116, 123, 124, 125, 127, 128, 130, 131, 133
employment, 15, 32, 79
encouragement, 32
enrollment, 20, 26, 40, 41, 42, 54, 55, 57, 63, 77, 85, 113
enthusiasm, 40
environment, 25, 26, 39, 76, 104, 125, 126, 127, 129
equities, 70, 74, 75, 84, 85, 90, 94
equity, 2, 3, 6, 37, 51, 77, 79, 81, 83, 84, 85, 86, 90, 91, 106
equity market, 82, 84
erosion, 66, 102
ethnicity, 49
execution, 19, 101, 109, 121
exercise, 108, 111
expenditures, 67, 69, 70, 71, 72
expertise, 47, 107
exposure, ix, 27, 48, 49, 60, 77, 83
extrapolation, 26, 29

F

failure, 41, 124
faith, 109
family, 34, 37, 40, 51, 52, 56, 98, 126, 128
fear, 36, 88, 104
federal law, 127
Federal Reserve Board, 4, 79
fiduciary responsibilities, 13, 103
finance, 25, 56, 60, 71, 121
financial crisis, ix, 28, 31, 47, 81, 88, 89, 90, 91, 93, 95, 97, 98
financial institutions, 26, 45, 65, 90, 132
financial markets, ix, 27, 34, 47, 49, 60, 67, 73, 74, 75, 77, 82
financial resources, 123
financial sector, 65
financing, 53, 57, 74
firms, 32, 42, 50, 54, 70, 72, 77, 89, 104, 108, 109, 110, 135
fiscal policy, 67
flexibility, 130
fluctuations, 77, 82
focusing, 81
food, 37, 87, 88
foreclosure, 43
freezing, 32, 81
fuel, 88
funding, ix, 1, 3, 7, 42, 52, 56, 57, 62, 74, 75, 81, 86, 89
funds, 2, 3, 4, 6, 12, 15, 19, 21, 22, 26, 34, 40, 41, 45, 46, 49, 51, 55, 57, 59, 60, 66, 67, 70, 74, 75, 77, 79, 84, 85, 87, 88, 90, 91, 94, 95, 99, 106, 107, 108, 109, 110, 111, 112, 113, 114, 115, 116, 118, 121, 124, 125, 126, 127, 128, 129, 130, 132, 136

G

GE, 61
gender, 49
general education, 113
generation, 31, 50
goals, 48
goods and services, 75, 111
governance, 102, 103, 106, 107
government, vi, 3, 12, 28, 31, 32, 33, 34, 36, 45, 55, 56, 57, 60, 65, 66, 67, 68, 71, 72, 94, 126, 127, 131
grades, 129
Great Depression, 97
greed, 97
groups, 18, 40, 41, 49, 69, 76, 79, 83, 84, 85, 130
growth, 5, 7, 26, 59, 65, 68, 71, 113
growth rate, 71
GS, 62
guidance, 28, 34, 42, 120
guidelines, 17

H

harm, 104
health, 35, 37, 45, 52, 69, 81, 87, 88, 99, 102, 117
health care, 37, 52, 69, 87, 102
health insurance, 45
hedging, 28
high school, 42
hiring, 75, 130
home value, 48
homeowners, 93, 97
hopes, 36
hospitalization, 88
House, vii, viii, x, 25, 31, 37, 47, 63, 65, 73, 74, 78, 81, 87, 89, 93, 97, 101, 106, 110, 123, 135, 136
households, ix, 17, 35, 51, 52, 53, 58, 67, 75, 76, 77
housing, 37, 51, 52, 73, 94, 98
human resources, 70
husband, 87

I

ideal, 53, 54
ideals, 103, 109
idiosyncratic, 55
image, 111
images, 37, 42
implementation, 85
impulsive, 26
incentives, 12, 33, 36,47, 48, 49, 54, 55, 63, 104
income, ix, 1, 3, 4, 7, 14, 15, 17, 22, 27, 28, 29, 32, 33, 34, 35, 36, 37, 40, 45, 46, 47, 50, 51, 52, 53, 54, 55, 57, 58, 60, 66, 67, 68, 69, 70, 71, 75, 76, 77, 81, 82, 85, 86, 87, 88, 89, 90, 94, 98, 99, 102, 103, 104, 105, 107, 114, 117, 119, 120, 125, 126, 130
income distribution, 77
income tax, 40, 57, 70, 71, 76
indexing, 109
indication, 59
industry, 3, 6, 7, 11, 15, 28, 59, 89, 98, 102, 103, 104, 105, 108, 116, 119, 120, 126, 127, 128, 129, 130, 131, 132
inefficiencies, 59
inefficiency, 67
inertia, 26, 63, 129
inflation, 28, 65, 66, 67, 71, 90
injury, vi, 58
insecurity, 88, 94
insight, 72, 89
institutions, 45, 73, 91
instruments, 28, 74
insurance, 4, 6, 13, 15, 28, 31, 37, 41, 58, 90, 91, 106, 116, 117, 120, 126, 127, 129
integrity, 18, 101
interbank market, 73
interest rates, 73, 74
intermediaries, 115
Internal Revenue Service, 15, 17
investors, ix, 12, 15, 21, 26, 48, 49, 56, 71, 94, 98, 108, 110, 118, 126, 133

J

JE, 61
jobs, 26, 27, 33, 34, 36, 53, 71, 123
jurisdiction, 109

L

labor, 42, 51, 77
labor force, 77
labor force participation, 77
language, 40, 42, 131
laws, 76, 89, 105, 107, 123, 124
lawyers, 130
leakage, 53, 55, 71, 84
legislation, x, 17, 37, 46, 48, 95
leisure, 69
lending, 73
lens, 103, 120
life expectancy, 36, 58
lifetime, 29, 34, 36, 55, 67, 95, 99
line, 88, 126
living standards, 58
loans, 11, 18, 40, 42, 51, 56, 73, 86, 87, 94, 98, 118
lobbying, 107
lobbyists, 72, 99
local government, 53, 55, 75
logistics, 129
longevity, 28, 33, 55
long-term care insurance, 117
love, 113
loyalty, 110

M

management, 4, 7, 15, 21, 39, 42, 45, 53, 59, 60, 98, 102, 111, 116, 117, 119, 121, 124, 126, 127, 131, 132, 136
mandates, 136
manufacturing, 40
market, ix, 20, 22, 25, 26, 28, 31, 33, 34, 36, 39, 40, 41, 43, 46, 48, 51, 55, 59, 73, 74, 75, 76, 77, 82, 83, 86, 90, 91, 98, 106, 109, 125, 130, 133
market penetration, 40
market segment, 55
marketing, 9, 111, 120, 126, 128, 129
marketplace, 41, 42, 127
markets, 25, 29, 34, 66, 73, 77, 98, 99, 119
measures, 98, 99, 131
median, 7, 33, 35, 53, 54, 55, 56, 58, 82, 86, 125
Medicare, 69
membership, 87
men, 40, 49
messages, 104
Mexico, 67, 121
MI, 62
mid-career, 82
middle class, 66
middle-class families, 37, 55
minimum wage, 66
minorities, 54, 60
minority, 118
model, 48, 53, 59, 82, 131
models, 85
money, ix, 6, 8, 13, 25, 26, 33, 34, 36, 40, 42, 45, 46, 48, 52, 53, 55, 58, 67, 69, 70, 71, 74, 91, 94, 99, 102, 106, 109, 111, 113, 121, 123, 124, 125, 126, 127, 128, 129, 130, 131, 132
moral hazard, 67
morning, 39, 93
mortality, 22, 117
motives, 104
movement, 48
myopia, 26

N

nation, 31, 34, 66, 67, 69, 70, 89, 95, 98, 99, 105, 106, 131, 132, 133
national income, 69
net investment, 126
newspapers, 133
normal goods, 69

O

objectives, 107, 114
objectivity, 12, 14, 128
Office of Management and Budget, 68
older people, 69
opacity, 73
opportunity costs, 125
order, 2, 3, 13, 40, 48, 58, 65, 73, 86, 109, 114
oversight, 3, 4, 12, 14, 95, 97, 102, 104, 110, 111, 120
overtime, 28
ownership, 114

P

pain, 42, 90
partnership, 45
passive, 106, 109, 118
payroll, 54, 87
pension plans, 2, 3, 4, 32, 33, 34, 36, 48, 55, 56, 59, 69, 72, 74, 75, 76, 77, 81, 94, 98, 99, 102, 123
pensions, 22, 32, 33, 34, 35, 37, 68, 69, 72, 73, 74, 76, 77, 94, 95, 99
performers, 83
planning, 32, 33, 34, 87
pneumonia, 88
policy makers, 12
policy responses, 48
polling, 52
pools, 15, 131
poor, 33, 35, 103, 129, 130
poor performance, 129
population, 33, 76, 98
portability, 56, 69
portfolio, 9, 20, 26, 59, 75, 105, 106, 107, 110, 114
portfolios, 26, 41, 59, 77, 106, 121
poultry, 69
poverty, 37
power, 124
PP, 61
preference, 41
premiums, 88
pressure, 42, 67
price changes, 59, 77
prices, 48, 49, 51, 65, 74, 75, 76, 118
private firms, 36
private investment, 32
private sector, 28, 41, 42, 50, 53, 94
producers, 132
professional management, 59
profit, 4, 37, 45, 63, 71, 102, 120, 123, 126, 128, 131
profits, 45, 65, 70, 71, 74
program, 25, 27, 28, 40, 41, 42, 55,62, 74, 102
proliferation, 115
property taxes, 88
protocol, 42
psychology, 48
public opinion, 52
public pension, 56, 75, 76
public policy, 47, 53, 104
public sector, 39, 55, 71
public service, 56
public support, 49

Q

quartile, 50, 82, 86

R

race, 49
range, 2, 3, 7, 12, 42, 45, 59, 60,67, 71, 85, 117
rate of return, 15, 57, 66, 67, 71, 125, 126, 132
ratings, 46
real estate, 51, 75, 91, 94
reality, 66, 91, 124, 132
reason, 34, 35, 83, 84, 109, 130
recall, 125
recession, 66, 67, 71, 99
recovery, 40
reflection, 36
reforms, 35, 36

regulation, 14, 20, 66, 103, 104, 110, 128, 130
regulations, 14, 20, 23, 99, 126, 131
regulators, 4, 28, 29, 98, 108
relationship, 40, 74, 115
relevance, 77
relief, 15, 31, 45, 46
replacement rate, 66, 82, 86
Requirements, 16
resources, 75, 116
retail, 12, 70, 111
retirement age, 53, 55, 77, 85, 98
retirement pension, 32
returns, 10, 12, 17, 26, 31, 34, 57, 62, 67, 76, 81, 86, 90, 107, 109, 119, 124, 125, 126, 136
revenue, 66, 102, 107, 108, 110, 114, 115, 116, 120, 121, 132
risk, ix, 1, 2, 3, 7, 11, 14, 21, 26, 28, 31, 32, 33, 34, 35, 36, 41, 45, 49, 55, 57, 58, 59, 60, 67, 71, 73, 77, 89, 90, 91, 102, 107, 117, 135
risk management, 57
risk profile, 14
RP, 61

S

safety, 26, 31
sales, 19, 21, 42, 66, 102, 105, 110, 111, 115, 116, 117, 128, 129, 132
sanctions, 119
savings, ix, 1, 3, 4, 8, 14, 25, 26, 27, 28, 31, 32, 33, 34, 39, 41, 42, 48, 49, 51, 54, 55, 56, 57, 58, 60, 63, 65, 67, 68, 69, 70, 71, 72, 88, 89, 90, 93, 94, 95, 98, 99, 105, 120, 127
savings account, 54, 58
savings rate, 69
scaling, 66
scholarship, 45
scores, 40
search, 46, 71
searching, 28
Secretary of the Treasury, 74
securities, 4, 7, 9, 15, 73, 75, 90, 94, 108, 109, 111
Securities Exchange Act, 108, 110, 121
security, ix, 20, 21, 22, 25, 26, 27, 29, 31, 32, 33, 34, 35, 36, 37, 39, 44, 45, 46, 47, 48, 49, 51, 52, 53, 54, 55, 57, 60, 66, 67, 68, 70, 71, 73, 81, 97, 98, 99, 107, 114, 119, 135
selecting, 7, 9, 12, 105, 128
Senate, 62, 63, 120
separation, 132
service provider, 2, 3, 7, 8, 9, 12, 13, 14, 18, 19, 20, 21, 22, 104, 115, 116, 119, 120, 135, 136
severe stress, 77
shareholders, 75, 98, 110
shares, 11, 13, 77, 114, 115
sharing, 4, 37, 40, 71, 95, 102, 110, 114, 116, 117, 120, 123, 132
signs, 35, 59, 94, 98
silver, 48, 60
simulation, 82, 86
skills, 69
skimming, 105
smoothing, 57, 76
Social Security, 31, 32, 33, 34, 35, 36, 37, 48, 56, 57, 61, 62, 65, 66, 67, 68, 69, 70, 76
sole proprietor, 68
space, 46, 128
spectrum, 128, 132
speed, 51
Spring, 72
stability, 41, 123
standard of living, 35, 52
standards, 3, 15, 27, 103, 132
statistics, 40, 123
stimulus, 67
stock, 4, 6, 22, 25, 26, 27, 29, 33, 34, 36, 41, 45, 46, 49, 70, 71, 74, 77, 79, 84, 86, 90, 106, 107, 125, 133
stock price, 74, 79
strain, 94
strategies, 59, 71
strength, 60
stress, 73
stroke, 131

students, 42
subgroups, 77
subsidy, 66, 116
Sun, 37, 72
supply, 13, 88
susceptibility, 91
Switzerland, 61

T

tactics, 130
tax collection, 76
tax credit, 57
tax deduction, 71
tax increase, 68
teaching, 103
technological change, 68
telephone, 7
tenure, 82, 83, 84, 85
thinking, 26
thoughts, 42
time periods, 132
Title I, 110
TF, 61
total costs, 133
tracking, 7, 115
trade, 19, 40, 65, 109, 121
trade costs, 109
trading, 21, 40, 41, 106, 107, 108, 109, 111, 116, 117, 119, 129, 132
training, 116
transaction costs, 110
transactions, 18, 19, 109, 111
transformation, 33, 35
transparency, 18, 91, 94, 99, 119
transportation, 37
Treasury bills, 90
trust, 7, 15, 19, 21, 59, 102, 103, 104, 105, 106, 107, 108, 113, 114, 115, 116, 118, 120
turnover, 82, 84, 107, 109, 124, 129

U

UK, 59
uncertainty, 94, 104
unemployment, 94, 98
United States, ix, 22, 37, 53, 59, 61, 69, 79, 103, 114
universe, 9, 10, 14, 15, 26, 33, 54, 84, 128, 130
university education, 87
updating, 14

V

variables, 85
vehicles, 33, 41, 45, 67, 69, 108, 116, 120
vein, 130
voice, 39, 88, 126, 131, 133
volatile environment, 28
volatility, 26, 40, 41, 42, 49, 81,83, 84, 116, 133
voters, 63
vulnerability, 55, 84

W

wages, 32, 94, 98, 102
WB, 61
wealth, 34, 35, 39, 48, 49, 50, 51, 52, 54, 55, 67, 75, 98, 106
withdrawal, 43, 56, 82, 94
witnesses, 95, 99
World War I, 35
worry, 52, 129
writing, 115, 116

Z

zero sum game, 126